Kipling's Hidden Narratives

*To my parents
and to
Lysbeth, Sue and Tony*

SANDRA KEMP

Kipling's
Hidden Narratives

Basil Blackwell

Copyright © Sandra Kemp 1988

First published 1988

Basil Blackwell Ltd
108 Cowley Road, Oxford, OX4 1JF, UK

Basil Blackwell Inc.
432 Park Avenue South, Suite 1503
New York, NY 10016, USA

British Library Cataloguing in Publication Data
Kemp, Sandra
    Kipling's hidden narratives.
    1. Kipling, Rudyard — Criticism and
    interpretation
    I. Title
    823'.8   PR4857
    ISBN 0-631-15577-5

Library of Congress Cataloging in Publication Data
Kemp, Sandra.
    Kipling's hidden narratives.
    Bibliography: p.
    Includes index.
    1. Kipling, Rudyard, 1865–1936—Criticism and
interpretation.   2. Identity (Psychology) in literature.
3. East and West in literature.   4. Narration (Rhetoric)
I. Title.
PR4858.135K4   1988   823'.8   87-34126
ISBN 0-631-15577-5

Typeset in 11 on 13pt Baskerville
by Downdell Limited, Oxford
Printed and bound in Great Britain
by T.J. Press Ltd, Padstow, Cornwall

It was a long afternoon crowded with mad episodes that rose and dissolved like the dust of our wheels; cross-sections of remote and incomprehensible lives through which we raced at right-angles; and I went home in the dusk, wearied out, to dream of . . . the steps of shy children in the wood, and the hands that clung to my knees as the motor began to move.

'They' (*TD*)

Contents

Acknowledgements

I would like to thank Julia Briggs, Frank Stack and Serena Surman for their help on an earlier version of this book as my doctoral thesis.

I am also very grateful to my editor Stephan Chambers, and to Richard Cronin, Robert Cummings, Aidan Day, John Drakakis, George Kearns, Lisa Lewis, Ann Parry, Donald Mackenzie, and David Trotter who read and commented on parts of this book in typescript.

The staff of the Modern Papers Reading Room of the Bodleian Library and the Manuscripts Section of the University Sussex Library have been particularly helpful. I am also indebted to the National Trust, as copyright-holders in the Literary Estate of Rudyard Kipling; the British Library, including the India Office Library and Records; the Bancroft Library, University of California at Berkeley; the Department of Rare Books, Cornell University Library; the Kipling Collection, Dalhousie University Library; the Houghton Library, Harvard University; the Henry W. and Albert A. Berg Collection, and to the New York Public Library, Astor, Lenox and Tilden Foundations.

My deepest indebtedness is to Karina Williamson, and to my family, to whom this book is dedicated.

Bibliographical Note

Except where indicated, all references are to The Sussex Edition of *The Complete Works in Prose and Verse of Rudyard Kipling*, 34 vols (1937), and to *Rudyard Kipling's Verse, Definitive Edition* (1940). Kipling himself supervised the preparation of the Sussex Edition, and the Definitive Edition of the poems is based on *Kipling's Collected Verse, 1885–1932* (1933), also prepared for publication by Kipling. There is a significant difference in the arrangement of stories (particularly in the early volumes) between the Sussex Edition and standard American edition – the Outward Bound. Kipling contextualized stories by their location within the volumes. The rearrangement of stories in the Outward Bound necessarily distorts this.

The works are abbreviated in the text as follows:

PTH	*Plain Tales from the Hills*
ST	*Soldiers Three*
WWW	*Wee Willie Winkie*
LH	*Life's Handicap*
MI	*Many Inventions*
TDW	*The Day's Work*
TD	*Traffics and Discoveries*
AR	*Actions and Reactions*
ADC	*A Diversity of Creatures*
DC	*Debits and Credits*
LR	*Limits and Renewals*
JB	*Jungle Book* and *Second Jungle Book*

JSS	*Just So Stories*
PPH	*Puck of Pook's Hill*
RF	*Rewards and Fairies*
LST and *TSD*	*Land and Sea Tales* and *Thy Servant a Dog*
SC	*Stalky and Co*
TLF	*The Light that Failed*
TN	*The Naulahka*
CC	*Captains Courageous*
Kim	*Kim*
FSS	*From Sea to Sea* (2 vols)
LT	*Letters of Travel*
ABW	*A Book of Words*
TW and *AFB*	*The War* and *A Fleet in Being*
IG	*The Irish Guards* (2 vols)
UP	*Uncollected Prose* (2 vols)
DD and *BRB*	*Departmental Ditties* and *Barrack-Room Ballads*
SS, FN and *YB*	*The Seven Seas, The Five Nations* and *The Years Between*
SFB and *LSFB*	*Songs from Books* and *Later Songs from Books*
DE	*Rudyard Kipling's Verse, Definitive Edition*

Introduction

'Oh God! Life had always been one long innuendo!' says Kipling's protagonist in 'Dayspring Mishandled' (*LR*). It is a remark that might equally apply to the construction of the story itself. On the surface his stories seem extroverted. But the different kinds of textuality at work in 'Dayspring Mishandled' – reticence, tonal change and oblique and multiple narration – are characteristic of most of his writings. In *Kim* Kipling himself acknowledged at least 'two/Separate sides to my head' and from *Plain Tales from the Hills*, the first collection of stories, to *Limits and Renewals*, the last, the stories reveal a continuing exploration of the way narrative makes and unmakes identity. The notion of a psyche assuming a repertoire of roles in order to confirm its own existence is a concern he shared with the Modernist writers to whom he is commonly opposed. When examined closely, the covert narrative sequences and self-reflexivity of his stories reveal strikingly Modernist tendencies.[1] In Kipling's case, however, the destabilization of narrative is informed by an immersion in Eastern thought. He spent formative years of his life in India and his stories interrogate the 'other self' of his childhood.

In later life, though his writings were still widely read, Kipling's name came to be more closely associated with a particular political attitude than with a set of stories and poems.[2] One of the problems in reading Kipling today is that the 'control' exercised over his stories by contemporary journal reviewers set limits upon Kipling's writings from which they are not yet free. Ann Parry has suggested that such reviews excluded possibilities in the stories that did not accord with Imperialist ideology (1985,

p. 256). Her study demonstrates the power of the late Victorian periodical press to regulate dominant ideas and values. She shows some of the ways in which journals attempted to supervise the encounter between reader and text, to assume (as John Morley put it in the *Fortnightly Review* of 1867) 'the momentous task of forming national opinion'. Reviews such as Andrew Lang and Edmund Gosse were particularly keen to recuperate Kipling's 'masculinity' from an increasing 'feminization' of literature – from what Gosse described as an absorption in 'the burrows of self-consciousness . . . and an excess of psychological analysis [and of] superhuman romance'. Reviewers like Lang and Gosse stereotyped the stories and over-emphasized their assertion of European ideas and values.[3]

In later life, Kipling himself became an outspoken commentator on political affairs. He strongly opposed Indian Nationalism, and worked with his cousin Stanley Baldwin on key political speeches. But if the public figure Kipling co-operated with the radical right-wing, the writer could not. Kipling's stories draw attention to politics, the Raj, the life of the common soldier and the business of trades and professions. But they also return compulsively to the ways in which identity is created by faith and superstition, by psychic and paranormal experience, by trauma, and by a pre-occupation with art and the agency of inspiration.

'Baa Baa, Black Sheep', Kipling's semi-autobiographical account of childhood, reveals some of these recurrent preoccupations. The story dramatizes the difference between the worlds of East and West, and the contrasting attitudes to subjectivity, language and narrative ascribed to them. It begins by setting a vision of the undisciplined yet loving and secure atmosphere of an upbringing in India against the narrow constraints of an English household ruled by extreme evangelical fervour. The narrative records the 'punishments and humiliations . . . above all humiliations' endured by a small child in the name of Christian instruction, his rebellion and eventual breakdown. As Punch, 'unquestioned despot of the house at Bombay', is transformed into the English Black Sheep, 'Child of the Devil and the inheritor of undying flame', he becomes angry, duplicitous, fearful and defiant. The difference between the two worlds is partly articulated through their contrasting attitudes to narrative. Aunty Rosa accepts that it is her duty to teach Punch to read, but refuses to help him understand the stories:

> 'What is a "falchion"? What is a "e-wee lamb"? What is a "base *us*surper"? What is a "verdant me-ad"?' he demanded, with flushed cheeks at bedtime, of the astonished Aunty Rosa.
> 'Say your prayers and go to sleep', she replied.

By contrast, those who surrounded Punch in the house at Bombay had half-created, and participated in, the tales they told him. 'The *hamal* made tiger-noises in twenty different keys.'

The narrative takes the form of a series of puzzles and questions as Punch attempts to make sense of the new life in terms of the old. 'But p'raps she's a new white *ayah*', he muses at the beginning: 'I'm to call her Antirosa, but she doesn't call *me* Sahib.' 'What is Antirosa?' he asks his little sister Judy. Later, when Punch obligingly attempts to integrate the Christian story of creation with what he can remember of his Indian fairy tales he is punished for it. Both children are perplexed by a caste system very different from the one with which they are familiar and by the unheard-of experiences of anger and corporal punishment. The series of cultural and spiritual dislocations reaches a climax in Punch's response to Uncle Harry's death. Like William in 'The Debt' (*LR*) and Tod in 'Tod's Amendment' (*PTH*), 'there were few details of wedding or burial that he had not known since he could ask questions', and Punch is not surprised by the news that Uncle Harry will soon be dead. ' "I'm very sorry", said Black Sheep soberly. "He told me a long time ago." ' When the dying man sings the Song of the Battle of Navarino for the last time Punch's immediate but unacknowledged perception is that this single moment of intense experience is something that will survive: ' "That day at Navarino, Uncle Harry!" ' shouted Black Sheep, half-wild with excitement and fear of he knew not what.' Like the narrator in 'Wireless' (*TD*), he responds at some unconscious level and his celebration of death, his intimations of a principle of reincarnation, contrast strongly with the misery and anger of Aunty Rosa, who cannot see beyond the immediate finality: 'Uncle Harry is *dead*', she screams at him.

The most distressing feature of Punch's new world is 'an abstraction called God' who becomes one of the story's main characters. Small though he is, Punch discerns a puzzling 'pettiness' and a contradictoriness in God's actions and reactions, and in the way his worshippers address him. 'Mamma's own prayer was a slightly illogical one. Summarized it ran: "Let strangers love my children and be as good to them as I should be, but let me preserve their love and their confidence for ever and ever." '

In 'Baa Baa, Black Sheep' the discrepancy between the two cultures justifies the narrator's claim that the children have 'lost all their world' and exemplifies the epigraph from Thompson's 'The City of Dreadful Night':

> Ah, well-a-day, for we are souls bereaved!
> Of all the creatures under Heaven's wide scope
> We are most hopeless, who had once most hope,
> And most beliefless, who had most believed.[4]

The children's initial feeling that their parents 'forgot' to take them with them when they left becomes a conviction that they have been 'abandoned indeed', and that 'Aunty Rosa' is acting under 'secret orders' from the absent parents. Punch's response is duplicity: 'plotting . . . a tangled web of deception that he wrapped around Aunty Rosa . . . he set his child's wits against hers and was no more beaten.' Years later in his autobiography, Kipling described the system of lying that he had developed during his own childhood as 'the foundation of literary effort'. He added:

> Nor was my life [at Southsea] an unsuitable preparation for my future, in that it demanded constant wariness, the habit of observation, and attendance on moods and tempers; the noting of discrepancies between speech and action; a certain reserve of demeanour; and an automatic suspicion of sudden favours . . . badly treated children have a clear notion of what they are likely to get if they betray the secrets of the prison house before they are clear of it. (1937, pp. 6, 15–16)[5]

In 'Baa Baa, Black Sheep' the pattern of fear, isolation and punishment which transforms the undisciplined but well-meaning child into a potential murderer re-inforces the cultural dislocation experienced by the children:

> 'It's all wrong,' said Harry magisterially. 'You nearly killed him, and I shouldn't wonder if he dies.'
> 'Will he die?' said Black Sheep.
> 'I daresay,' said Harry, 'and then you'll be hanged and go to hell.'
> 'All right,' said Black Sheep, picking up the table-knife. 'Then I'll kill *you* now. You may say things and do things – and I don't know how things happen, and you never leave me alone – and I don't care *what* happens!' He ran at the boy with the knife.

The narrative makes it clear that Punch's behaviour does not merit the 'tortures physical and psychical' devised by Aunty Rosa, her son Harry and her 'intimate friend and ally', God. It sets their inflated religious vocabulary ('possession by the Devil', 'depraved mind') against Uncle Harry's dispassionate statement that 'he's a good enough little chap'. At the end of the story Punch withdraws into a world of terrifying shadow-shapes and extreme mental isolation: 'he grew afraid of the shadows of window-curtains and the flapping of doors and the creaking of shutters . . . [in] the garden . . . the rustle of the laurel bushes frightened him.' His breakdown introduces the subjects – pathological isolation, sympathy for social misfits and outcasts, unmerited suffering and of darkness turning to blindness – which recur in Kipling's work.

> 'There! Told you so,' says Punch. 'It's all different now, and we are just as much Mother's as if she had never gone.'
> Not altogether, O Punch, for when young lips have drunk deep of the bitter waters of Hate, Suspicion, and Despair, all the Love in the world will not wholly take away that knowledge; though it may turn darkened eyes for a while to the light, and teach Faith where no Faith was.

Throughout his writings Kipling seems to be searching for a structure of belief that would recognize the reality of both love and hate, and the reality of their co-existence. 'So close must any

life-filling passion lie to its opposite', he tells us in his autobiography (1937, p. 16).

Kipling's 'hidden narratives', then, are caught between conflicting modes of perception. The conflict between inner and
outer, or between individual and society, generates the four
connected but distinguishable concerns that are the subject of this
book. *Kipling's Hidden Narratives* is not primarily a theoretical or
contextual study, but offers an exploration of these hidden and
unexpected preoccupations which revise the accepted view of
Kipling's writings.

There are, in the first place, stories that explore subjectivity in
its relation to cultural codes that are perceived to be contingent and
relative. 'Baa Baa, Black Sheep' is perhaps flawed by Kipling's
undue insistence that we take sides with Punch. His early stories
do define India as an unknown other in the terms established by
a European racism which ignores process and history.[6] But
ambivalent or multiple perspectives undermine their assertion
of a colonialist will to power and knowledge.

Kipling also explored the ambivalent or multiple bases of narrative voice. He wrote under more than thirty pseudonyms, and it
is not just his ability (in his own words) 'to think in another man's
skin' that is at issue, but what John Bayley describes as a 'compart-
mented mind': 'As in Browning's metaphor in *Love in a Life* . . .
we go from room to room through closed doors . . . we experience
contradictions and prejudices which do not meet and examine
each other except through our presence' (Bayley, 1976, p. 56).
This would account for the peculiar divisions of voice and vocabulary that haunt Kipling's writings: victim *and* persecutor; the
language of trades, professions and the gentleman's club *and* the
discourse of dream, drugs and insanity. Popular – even clichéd –
themes in Kipling are treated in a highly wrought and intricately
textured manner. But there is no way of resolving the conflict of
voices by reference to authorial intention. Like Browning's Fra
Lippo Lippi, whom he considered 'not too remote ancestor',
Kipling gets 'caught up' in his own art 'by mistake'. He is at
once outside and inside, safely distanced by an encircling frame
and suitably anonymous narrator, yet imprisoned within and
endangered by the text at the same time. This is perhaps what

W. H. Auden means when he speaks of 'The anxiety of encirclement from both within and without' in Kipling's writing (Auden
1943, p. 579).

The third preoccupation concerns the narrative function of lies,
secrecy and silence. A distinction between story (events in their
chronological order) and plot (the story as it is actually told) is
insufficient here. Kipling's plots are frequently cut across by
materialist or historical discourses – the 'languages' of Imperialism, of medicine or of religion. Thus a plot of recognizable shape
or type (for example, a detective story) may be interrupted by a
discourse (for example, that of psychoanalysis) that does not
obviously fit that plot. The result is a narrative effect that cannot
be defined in terms of story or plot. In 'Baa Baa, Black Sheep',
reticence and repression are creative as well as childish. In 'False
Dawn' (*PTH*) Kipling's narrator, like Marlow in Conrad's *Heart
of Darkness*, can only tell his story 'in the dark'; and his counterpart in 'By Word of Mouth' (*PTH*) also abdicates responsibility:
'This tale may be explained by those who know how souls are
made and where the bounds of the possible are put down. I have
lived long enough in this India to know that it is best to know
nothing and can only write the story as it happened.' Another
kind of narrator conceals his or her motive behind some surface
appearance or explanation (as in 'A Madonna of the Trenches',
DC). What is left unsaid in Kipling's narratives becomes as important as what is stated. A telling metaphor for this narrative
technique is to be found in the narrator's description of the dour
Australian sheep-farmer, Hickmot, in 'A Friend of the Family'
(*DC*): 'If he was noticeable, it was on account of his unnotice-
ability – same way you'd notice there not being an extra step at
the bottom of the staircase when you thought there was.'

Finally, Kipling also explored the source of literature and of the
self in states of madness and breakdown. Like Punch's 'night
terrors' and blindness in 'Baa Baa, Black Sheep's and Pansay's
'ghastly and yet in some indefinable way . . . marvellously dear
experience' in 'The Phantom Rickshaw' (*WWW*), Kipling's
stories frequently enter states outside linguistic and rational
control. The tight construction of the short story, and the conse-
quent density of its language, encourage suggestion and allusion.

Both reference out of the text, and the foregrounding of images within it, conspire to resist interpretation and integration (Hanson, 1985, p. 4). In a number of stories Kipling presents the agency of inspiration in terms of the powers and techniques of the doctor and of the detective: acting as writers of special competence these practitioners unravel stories from images of the dark and diseased territories of the mind. Elsewhere, Kipling's fascination with 'the Dark Places' is also associated with the power of sexuality, language and gender. Women, in Kipling's stories, like the indigenous population of India, may at points be subjected to what Bhabha describes as 'a narrative economy of voyeurism and fetishism' (1986, p. 153). But once again it is often hard to speak of a univocal narrative stance when it comes to Kipling's treatment of women. In retrospect, Max Beerbohm's famous attack, in which he pretends that 'Rudyard Kipling' is the pseudonym of a female author, is curiously suggestive (1943, p. 56). It is not often enough noted how frequently Kipling assumes a woman's voice, and, especially in the late stories, the way he privileges distinctly 'feminine' sensibilities. 'What is a God beside Woman?' asks the speaker in the poem that prefaces 'The Wish House' (*DC*). To which the answer: 'Dust and derision'. In this story the progress of Grace Ashcroft's narrative is inextricably linked with a child's demand for belief and trust in the irrational and in the imaginary (the trust in 'the wish house'). But here, as throughout Kipling's writings, the hidden narratives locate a domain where the need to acknowledge disturbance of mind is inseparable from the supernatural and curative powers of art. 'The main point', as the doctor, Keede, concludes in 'Unprofessional' (*LR*), 'is that it makes one not so much think . . . as imagine a bit.'

Notes

1   For a working definition of Modernism see Friedman (1981) pp. 97–8: 'The starting point of modernism is the crisis of belief that pervades twentieth century western culture: loss of faith, experience of fragmentation and disintegration, and the shattering of cultural symbols and norms. At the centre of this crisis were the new tech-

nologies of science, the epistemology of logical positivism, and the relativism of functionalist thought – in short, major aspects of the philosophical perspectives that Freud embodied. The rationalism of science and philosophy attacked the validity of traditional religious and artistic symbols while the growing technology of the industrialized world produced the catastrophes of war on the one hand and the atomization of human beings on the other. Art produced after the first world war recorded the emotional aspect of this crisis; despair, hopelessness, paralysis, angst, and a sense of meaninglessness, chaos and the fragmentation of material reality. In a variety of ways suited to their own religious, literary, mythological, occult, political, or existentialist perspectives, artists emerged from the paralysis of absolute despair to an active search for meaning. The search for order and pattern began in its own negation, in the overwhelming sense of disorder and fragmentation caused by the modern materialist world. The artist as seer would attempt to create what the culture could no longer produce: symbol and meaning in the dimension of art, brought into being through the agency of language, the Word or Logos of the twentieth century.' See White (1976) for a fascinating discussion of 'obscurity' in three early modernists – George Meredith, Henry James and Joseph Conrad – whose writings bear significant comparison with Kipling.

2   For a study of the critical reception of Kipling's writings see Rouse (1964).

3   For reviews of Kipling's writings see Green (1971).

4   First published in *National Reformer*, 1874. Reprinted in Messenger and Watson (1974).

5   Kipling was sent to England at the age of six to live at Lorne Lodge in Southsea, the home of Captain and Mrs Holloway. For biographical information see Carrington (1955) and Birkenhead (1980).

6   Edward Said's work on 'Orientalism' (1978) examines the discourses that have mediated and produced the West's relationship with the East. For an analysis of Kipling and 'Orientalism' see Moore-Gilbert (1986). For theories of colonial discourse see Bhabha (1984, 1985, 1986); Fanon (1965, 1970); and JanMohamed (1983). It is not the purpose of this book to examine Kipling's troubled production of knowledge of India.

1

'Two . . . sides to my head':
Divided identity in the Indian stories

'As one turns over the pages of his *Plain Tales from the Hills* one feels as if one were seated under a palm-tree reading life by superb flashes of vulgarity' wrote Oscar Wilde of Kipling's first collection of stories (Wilde, 1890, p. 104). 'Life', in *Plain Tales* and the other collections (*Wee Willie Winkie, Life's Handicap, Many Inventions, Kim, The Jungle Books* and *The Day's Work*), turns out to mean the activities of the Raj and the work of Empire. In all these stories the knowing and detached journalistic voice is at pains to assure us that its job is merely descriptive: 'the climate and the work are against playing tricks with words', it tells us ('The Conversion of Aurelian McGoggin', *PTH*). At the same time, however, the task of interpreting India authoritatively is undermined by the fluidity of the self which interprets and commands. In *Kim* the express search for identity structures the action: 'Who is Kim-Kim-Kim?' asks the eponymous hero. The image of the locked and unlocked cog-wheel encapsulates the interweaving of private and public self:

> All that while he felt, though he could not put it into words, that his soul was out of gear with its surroundings – a cog-wheel unconnected with any machinery, just like the idle cog-wheel of a cheap Beheea sugar-crusher laid by in a corner. The breezes fanned over him, the parrots shrieked at him, the noises of the populated house behind – squabbles, orders, reproofs – hit on dead ears . . . He did not want to cry, – had never felt less like crying in his life, – but of a sudden easy, stupid tears trickled down his nose, and with

an almost audible click he felt the wheels of his being lock up anew on the world without. Things that rode meaningless on the eye an instant before slid into proper proportion. Roads were meant to be walked on, houses to be lived in, cattle to be driven, fields to be tilled, and men and women to be talked to. They were all real and true – solidly planted upon the feet – perfectly comprehensible – clay of his clay, neither more nor less.

In *The Jungle Books* Mowgli is similarly caught between dual 'realities': 'As Mang the Bat flies between the beasts and birds so fly I between the village and the Jungle.' But there is more to this duality. If both village and jungle are subject to a highly codified 'Law', they also incorporate irreducibly lawless energies. It is a lawlessness which Daniel Karlin sees embodied in the 'feckless play' of the Bandar-log: 'inventing or appropriating a series of identities . . . They live from day to day, without law, without memory; they embody, if you like, that part of our nature whose floating, irresponsible and self-absorbed energy is at odds with the principle of ordered and controlled design, a threat to the ordered discourse of the Jungle' (1987, pp. 16, 24). In 'The Bridge Builders' (*TDW*) this threat becomes even more apparent in the split between narrative modes within the story. The precise realism of the description of bridge-building and other activities at the outset contrasts with the surreal or fantastic account of the opium trance at the end. In *Plain Tales*, the witty and cynical narrative voice reveals the same desire both to maintain and to abandon a fixed identity. So these stories are also characterized by perspectival shifts between inner and outer, inaction and participation, and between Indian and English words and values. In 'Beyond the Pale', for example, the contrast is simply expressed in terms of 'daytime' and 'night' worlds:

In the day-time, Trejago drove through his routine of office-work or put on his calling clothes and called on the ladies of the Station . . . At night, when the City was still, came the walk under the evil-smelling *boorka*, the patrol through Jitha Megli's *bustee*, the quick turn into Amir Nath's Gully

between the sleeping cattle and the dead walls, and then last
of all Bisesa . . . his dearer, out-of-the-way life.

Elsewhere in *Plain Tales* the movement between public and
private, and between conscious and unconscious, is figured
through stories concerning disguised or mistaken identity. The
seemingly abandoned woman in 'His Wedded Wife' turns out to
be a young male subaltern seeking revenge; the horror and confusion of 'False Dawn' causes Saumarez to mistake one sister for
another and thus to propose to the wrong woman; the action of
'On the Strength of a Likeness' (*PTH*) turns on Hannasyde's
wilful treatment of Mrs Landys-Haggert as if she were the girl he
had once tried to marry. The story of 'The Arrest of Lieutenant
Golightly' (*PTH*) concerns confusion between a serving officer
and a deserter. The *faquir* in 'To be Filed for Reference' (*PTH*)
and the *sais* in 'Miss Youghil's Sais' (*PTH*) are respectively the
ex-Oxford don McIntosh Jellaludin and the British Policeman
Strickland who could pass for a 'native':

> He [Strickland] was perpetually 'going Fantee' among
> natives, which, of course no man with any sense believes in.
> He was initiated into the *Sat Bhai* at Allahabad once, when
> he was on leave; he knew the Lizard-Song of the Sansis, and
> the *Hálli-hukk* dance, which is a religious can-can. When a
> man knows the *Hálli-hukk* . . . He has gone deeper than the
> skin.

The effect of these dangerously fluid transitions between frames of
reference is to create narratives described in 'Bitters Neat' (*PTH*)
as 'all criss-cross' or 'tangled'. No single psychological or moral
perspective is consistently privileged or sustained. As Moriarty
discovers in the story 'In Error' (*PTH*), the process of revision
undermines too easy judgements about truth and reality, about
religious and ethical codes: 'He could not scale things properly or
see what was what.'

In Kipling's representations of India, the maintenance of appearances does not secure survival. His catch-phrase 'the night
got into my head' (1937, p. 53) describes the stories' constant fear
of disintegration. In each instance, the inner operations of 'the

unnerved brain' are conveyed through a resonance of descriptive detail which offers a kind of negative impression of a story hidden beneath the surface narrative. It is a method we might associate with the procedures of the French Symbolists, and is equally manifest in the surreal dimensions of the prose-poem Kipling slips unobtrusively into his autobiography:

> Once I faced the reflection of my own face in a jet-black mirror of the window-panes for five days. When the fog thinned, I looked out and saw a man standing opposite the pub where the bar-maid lived. Of a sudden his breast turned dull red like a robin's, and he crumpled having cut his throat. In a few minutes – seconds it seemed – a hand-ambulance arrived and took up the body. A pot-boy with a bucket of steaming water sluiced the blood off into the gutter, and what little crowd had collected went its way. (pp. 86–7)

Such haunting and disturbed perspectives feature as manifest signs of hidden fears in 'The Gate of the Hundred Sorrows' (*PTH*), 'The Strange Ride of Morrowbie Jukes' (*WWW*), 'The Dream of Duncan Parrenness' (*LH*) and 'At the End of the Passage' (*LH*). These stories betray a nervous susceptibility alert to menace: their pathologized world of want and despair is directly attributable to a vision of India.

'The Gate of the Hundred Sorrows' is a dramatic monologue spoken by a dying man in an opium trance. Like the places of mystic vision described in 'They' (*TD*) and in *Kim*, 'the Gate' is hard to find: 'You might even go through the very gully it stands in a hundred times, and be none the wiser', the narrator says. It is itself a transformation: a house rather than a gate, but nonetheless a gateway through time, an exit from daily routine. Concerned only with the present moment of watching the red and black dragons on the ornamental coffin 'move about and fight', the narrator imagines those around him to be 'hundreds and hundreds of years old'. In contrast to mystical moments in other stories, however, this one does not offer full release. As his monologue progresses the narrator becomes increasingly uncertain about the reality of past events, and less and less active: 'I couldn't do a day's work now to save my life', he says. But in other respects his perceptions remain acute and rooted in the material world. He is fully aware that after the death of Fung Tching the Joss is neglected: 'The Joss doesn't get so many sticks burnt under his nose as he used to . . . He's all brown, too, and no one ever attends to him'; he also notices that his own opium is mixed with glue; that the dragons have become 'all torn and dirty, like the mats', and, poignantly, that while Tsin-ling provided the old bazaar-woman with 'a clean mat' to die on, 'he took her bangles just the same'. As so often in Kipling, the way into the story lies through its epigraph: 'If I can obtain Heaven for a pice, why should you be envious?' Here, as in 'In the House of Suddhoo', 'the magic that is always demanding gifts is no true magic'. At the end, there is horror in the sustained agoraphobia and self-imposed imprisonment of the narrator: 'I should be afraid of dying in the open now', he says.

'The Strange Ride of Morrowbie Jukes' provides another form of death-in-life, but in this story narcotics are not necessary to induce the state. When Morrowbie Jukes falls into a pit in which Hindu outcasts are imprisoned, he finds himself literally among the living dead:

> Sixteen years ago, when I first landed in Bombay I had been told . . . of the existence, somewhere in India, of a place to which such Hindus as had the misfortune to recover from trance or catalepsy were conveyed and kept, and I recollect laughing heartily at what I was then pleased to consider a traveller's tale.

As Morrowbie Jukes experiences life reduced to bare essentials – 'To eat and fight and sleep till we die' – he comes to realize the fragility of the 'canon[s] of the world' by comparison with the pit beneath. Just before he is rescued he realizes that his own ethical criteria have broken down. 'Morality is blunted by consorting with the Dead who are alive', he says.

The story may be read as an imaginative presentation of what happens when the ruler joins the very lowest of the ruled. The narrator can claim that 'There is no invention about this tale', because India has provided its own terrors. At the same time, the

bizarre ingenuity of the plot, and the almost allegorical description
of the Hindu outcasts, 'aged to all appearances as the Fates themselves', suggests that anxieties may have been projected onto the
environment. In this sense the story is yet another exploration of
the evasive fabrications of the inner self. The narrator imagines
what it would be like to be alive in Hell:

> If it were possible to forejudge the conversation of the
> Damned on the advent of a new soul in their abode, I should
> say that they would speak as Gunga Dass did to me through-
> out that long afternoon. I was powerless to protect or answer;
> all my energies being devoted to a struggle against the inex-
> plicable terror that threatened to overwhelm me again and
> again. I can compare the feeling to nothing except the
> struggles of a man against the overpowering nausea of the
> Channel passage – only my agony was of the spirit and
> infinitely more terrible.

The naturalizing banality of this comparison is puzzling, yet
powerful. Although at the end of the story Jukes is rescued by his
servant Dunnoo, what lingers on in the imagination is the world
of the living dead. Jukes's anger at those who disbelieve his tale is
vividly described, but much of the power of the narrative derives
from the equivocal placing of the experience. Did the events of the
story take place in 'reality' or in 'imagination'?

'The Dream of Duncan Parrenness' is a variation on a similar
theme but in this story the avenging denizens of the pit are translated into a single figure, the narrator's own *doppelgänger*: a future
self whose face is his own 'but marked and lined and scarred with
the furrows of disease and much evil living'. The narrator falls
into a stupor after an evening's heavy drinking, and wakes to find
this figure sitting at the foot of his bed. It offers him the prospect
of a long life, including the Governorship of India, in exchange
for his soul, his conscience, and his trust in man and woman. The
terrible price would seem punishment enough for the fever-ridden
narrator, 'wasted by all the sicknesses of the past four months',
but after exacting it, the other self departs, leaving only 'a little
piece of dry bread'. As in 'The Gate of the Hundred Sorrows', in
this story the vision is mediated in terms of hidden anxieties. The

pathologized world of India again relates to the constitution of the other: 'this land had so burnt and seared my mind'.

In 'At the End of the Passage' the title signifies another gateway or exit from routine: heat, loneliness and overwork cause Hummil to see his double, as Duncan Parrenness had done. But in this story Kipling combines the *doppelgänger* theme with that of the radical disintegration of the personality into multiple or irreconcilable selves. Hummil's fate is imaginatively described by his native servant Chuma: 'Heaven-born, in my poor opinion, this that was my master has descended into the Dark Places, and there has been caught because he was not able to escape with sufficient speed.'

At the beginning of the story four men 'not conscious of any special regard for each other' meet to while away a hot Indian day: 'It was as though the earth were dying of apoplexy', the narrator says. As they play whist and poker in desultory fashion, their thoughts turn to Sundays at home, and their mood is reflected in the snatch of the evening hymn Mottram chooses to play on the piano:

> May no ill dreams disturb my rest,
> No powers of darkness me molest.

As the narrative continues, it becomes clear that the 'powers of darkness' imaged and feared in the evening hymn have invaded Hummil's mind.[1] His uncertain moods – or in the words of Spurstow, the doctor, 'his savage personalities' – suggest the processes of breakdown. Spurstow stays behind that evening to look after him, and discovers that Hummil is haunted by 'a blind face that cries and can't wipe its eyes, a blind face that chases him down corridors' in recurrent dreams. 'Put me quite to sleep', he begs the doctor, 'for if I'm caught I die'. Later on in the story the face combines with his *doppelgänger*, 'the figure of himself . . . standing on the verandah', to drive him out of his mind. Kipling describes the process of mental and spiritual fragmentation in an image that equates the world of the unconscious with the realm of childhood:

As a sponge rubs a slate clean, so some power unknown to

Spurstow had wiped out of Hummil's face all that stamped it
for the face of a man, and he stood at the doorway in the
expression of his lost innocence. He had slept back into terri-
fied childhood.

Here the association of the child with memory and myth creates
an anarchic subjective realm where the self is no longer shielded
from terror by adult frames of identity.

The child is always an important repository of suggestiveness
for Kipling. The sense of an archetype of childhood, and the
presence of the child behind Kipling's own creative impulse pervades the stories, and was the animus behind the *Puck* books and
Just So Stories. 'At the End of the Passage' and other Indian stories
imply a correspondence between the animistic eye of the small
child and certain supernatural beliefs. They create an archetype
of childhood – a valuation of the child*like* rather than a disparage-
ment of the child*ish*. The energies of childhood operate beyond
conscious memory and may vanish without trace. They cannot be
contained within any social or rational understanding.

In a number of stories in *Plain Tales from the Hills*, *Life's Handicap* and *Many Inventions* Kipling attributes the same kind of paranormal or even magical powers to the Indians. 'By Word of
Mouth', 'The Return of Imray' (*LH*) and 'The Lost Legion'
(*MI*) implicate identity in the supernatural and of the paranormal. These narratives are characteristically duplicitous and
equivocal; they relativize the European colonial discourse which
frames them. The European mind in Kipling's stories is not
securely rational; they work to expose the contingency and relativity of Western valuations of 'masculinity' and 'rationality'.

The duplicity of these stories lies in the treatment of imaginative, paranormal and supernatural potencies which elude the
fixing of cultural stereotyping. The domain of the supernatural –
of the *not known* of what we know only by negative prefixes, the
*ir*rational or the *un*canny – is the locus of possibilities that may
stand outside culturally determined identity. Kipling does not
always subscribe to a literal belief in the supernatural; but the
continuing dialectic between scepticism and belief in his writings
enables him to take the measure of that which cannot be measured.

In 'In the House of Suddhoo' and *Kim*, for example, supposedly supernatural demonstrations are exposed as mere trickery. Other stories reveal an equal scepticism with regard to the reputed paranormal activities of the native priests. In *Kim* the Lama laments the 'devildom, charms and idolatry' that have infiltrated the practices of his Lamassery:

> the immense and sumptuous ritual of avalanche-guarded cathedrals; of processions and devil-dances; of the changing of monks and nuns into swine; of holy cities fifteen thousand feet in the air; of intrigue between monastery and monastery; of voices among the hills, and of that mysterious mirage that dances on dry snow.

Elsewhere the grotesque leper priest of 'The Mark of the Beast' (*LH*), the dumb priest of Kyoh in 'The Sacrifice of Er-Heb' (*BRB*), the one-eyed priest of 'Bubbling Well Road' (*LH*) and the Sadhu who cuts off his tongue in 'Hunting a Miracle' (*FSS*) are shown to be reverenced merely on the principle that what cannot be understood must be a manifestation of the gods. In *The Naulahka* the native priest who disbands Kate's hospital is unknown to its inmates and 'half-mad', yet they do not question his authority: 'He is a holy man. He has worked miracles', they tell Kate.

In the same way Kipling's treatment of the 'Evil Eye' shows that the relationship between individuals in Indian culture involves feelings and moral constraints that are intellectually comprehensible but emotionally alien to the West (Husain, 1964, p. 62). As the viewpoints shift quickly and radically from East to West, the narratives become entangled with the author's fundamentally questioning imagination and are inseparable from his moral and spiritual preoccupations. In 'Without Benefit of Clergy' (*LH*) Ameera hangs up a black jar in order to avert the Evil Eye. In the same way, the Jat in *Kim* puts his little boy in girl's clothing and the Kulu woman will not listen to the praises of her children. The narrator in 'The Finances of the Gods' (*LH*) checks his natural impulse to praise the child for fear of the consequences; in 'The Return of Imray' Imray is murdered for his carelessness in this respect. The loyal servant Bahadur Khan, who kills Imray, is afraid but unrepentant, so powerful is his belief in the Evil Eye:

> 'He said he was a handsome child, and patted him on the head; wherefore my child died. Wherefore I killed Imray Sahib in the twilight . . .' Bahadur Khan stood ashen-grey in the light of the one lamp. The need for justification came upon him very swiftly. 'I am trapped,' he said, 'but the offence was that man's. He cast an evil eye upon my child, and I killed and hid him.'

Significantly, however, the extremes of passion here are viewed within the context of the European detective's more rational view of the case: 'Simply and solely through not knowing the nature of the Oriental, and the coincidence of a little seasonal fever'.

The same kind of shifts in moral perspective occur in 'One View of the Question' (*MI*) and 'On the City Wall' (*IBW*). Neither story concerns the supernatural, but both explore subtle discrepancies between story and discourse, the stated and the implicit. In each instance a probing exploration of identity undermines easy interpretation.

'One View of the Question' involves the reversal of the usual 'play' of discourses by constituting England and the English as 'other'. It takes the form of a letter from a Muslim visiting London to his brother in India. Shafiz Khan is horrified by what he sees: 'This place is far gone in rottenness . . . and forgotten of God', he writes. Throughout the narrative Shafiz Khan adopts a Swiftian persona. As a calm and reasonable man seeking as far as possible to ascertain the facts, he proceeds by explaining and exposing, always with the seemingly courteous intent that his brother, like himself, should both learn and understand: 'so greatly has the foot of travel let out the stirrup-holes of belief'. His reasonable questions would seem to demand reasonable answers and the narrative is punctuated by reflection and instruction. 'This is a thing to be put in the cupboard of the mind . . . This is a terror beyond the pen . . . Read here with a fresh mind after sleep, I write as I understand.' In contrast to the English, who openly call each other 'liars, dogs and bastards', Shafiz Khan stresses his love for his brother and his conviction of a shared bond: 'Heart speaks naked to Heart . . . Glory and Honour on thy house till the ending of the years and a tent in the borders of Paradise.'

Despite its protestations of 'Love and Sincerity', the language reveals the tension of violence beneath its surface calm: a power of response that is proud and egocentric. Intermingled with graphic descriptions of the spiritual destitution of London are exhortations, repeated three times, to plot the downfall of 'that jesting dog without teeth – Bahadur Shah'; and instructions to murder 'Durga Charan Laha, in Calcutta' and also the dismissed groom 'Futteh Lah', should the occasion present itself. Towards the English, Shafiz Khan reveals a 'Holy War' mentality. There is no question of conversion here. Given half a chance, he would wipe the English off the face of the earth. Elsewhere his restraint is equally sinister: 'I have heard these cattle speak as princes and I have laughed, but not altogether.' Like the English, Shafiz Khan too is 'at secret war and veiled killing'.

The letter is a fabric of 'uneasy words', and Shafiz Khan's description of the English as 'word-confounding' is equally applicable to himself as he acknowledges: 'My words and intentions are those of truth yet it may be that I write nothing but lies . . . But from the same clay two men will never fashion platters alike, nor from the same facts draw equal conclusions.' In this story, as in 'On the City Wall', the clue to inner meaning is to be found in the words of the song. 'Hadst thou not called it Love, I had said it were a drawn sword'. By the time Shafiz Khan comes to the end of his letter it is clear that he has indeed 'Rid[den] sideways at the wall of expression'.

In 'On the City Wall', the Muslim Wali Dad's conversion to Christianity, and the contrast drawn between the two religions, are also bound up with the nature of language. 'I cannot make an end to my sentence without quoting from your authors', complains Wali Dad to the narrator. This hampers him and contributes to his passivity and unreliability: during the riots he arrives too late to smuggle Khem Singh out of the city, and the narrator is tricked into taking his place. Throughout the narrative the English mode of communication – 'telegrams and newspapers' – is contrasted unfavourably with the language of the Indian bazaars: 'India has gossiped for centuries . . . "Don't speak English" ', Lalun says. She represents what Kipling conceives of as the inaccessibility of India. Her little house on the city wall contains 'all the city'. It is a place where 'tomorrow never came' and her timeless and riddling complexities undermine the simple and timebound truths of the Supreme Government. 'I choose to tell what I choose to tell', she says, and Wali Dad is intuitively in conspiracy with her. 'I belong to a nation of liars. Think for yourself.' Together Wali Dad and Lalun compose and sing the songs that form the fabric of the narrative and contain the clue to its interpretation. Like the Persian poetry they quote to each other 'with a triple pun in every line' their lyrics do not convey meaning openly but move alluringly round its surfaces:

> One song, the prettiest of all, says that the beauty of Lalun
> was so great that it troubled the hearts of the British Govern-
> ment and caused them to lose their peace of mind. That is
> the way the song is sung in the streets; but if you examine it
> carefully and know the key to the explanation, you will find
> that there are three puns in it – on 'beauty', 'heart' and
> 'peace of mind,' – so that it runs: 'By the subtlety of Lalun
> the administration of the Government was troubled and it
> lost such and such a man.'

As the familiar words set undermining ironies into play, the narrator increasingly becomes ensnared in his own story. 'Since I was then living this story not writing it', like his counterpart in 'False Dawn', he recognizes that 'the tale must be told from the outside – in the dark – all wrong'. He is the exact antithesis of Wali Dad, who speaks and writes in the English tradition but cannot 'live' in it, effectively confirming the implicit negative response to Khem Singh's wise rhetorical question: 'Will oil and water mix?' By the end of the story *both* the lapsed convert and the English narrator play 'Vizier' to Lalun's effortlessly triumphant 'Queen'. As Wali Dad had previously claimed: 'Lalun *is* Lalun, and when you have said that, you have come only to the beginnings of knowledge.'

'The Limitations of Pambé Serang' (*LH*) extends the consideration of cultural difference beyond European and Indian to

include that between two non-European characters. In this story
Pambé waits over a year at the Nyanza Docks to take his revenge
on an African stoker, Nurkeed, who once insulted him in a
drunken brawl. As he can only redeem his honour by killing
Nurkeed, 'time was no object to him', and the narrator describes
with irony how he turns Christian in order to support himself:

> When the money failed, a kind gentleman told Pambé to
> become a Christian: and Pambé became one with great
> speed, getting his religious teaching between ship and ship's
> arrival, and six or seven shilling a week for distributing
> tracts to mariners. What the faith was Pambé did not in the
> least care; but he knew if he said 'Native Ki-lis-tian, Sar' to
> men with long black coats he might get a few coppers.

However, he contracts pneumonia while waiting and is taken in
by the 'kind gentleman', who sets about nursing him back to
health. During his convalescence he hears Nurkeed's voice outside one day, and asks for him to be brought up. ' "How
beautiful," said the kind gentleman, "How these orientals love
like children." ' But Pambé kills Nurkeed as he bends over the
bed and then waits until he is 'sufficiently healthy to be hanged in
due and proper form'.

Throughout the story the narrator is at pains to emphasize that
Pambé is as impenetrable to Nurkeed as to the Englishman, and
his fear is chillingly rendered:

> At noon, when all the ship's lascars were feeding, Nurkeed
> advanced into their midst, and being a placid man with a
> large regard for his own skin, he opened negotiations . . .
> Their faces immediately dropped all expression, as is the
> custom of the Oriental when there is killing on the carpet or
> any chance of trouble. Nurkeed looked long at the white eye-
> balls. He was only an African, and could not read character.
> A big sigh – almost a groan – broke from him, and he went
> back to the furnaces . . . Nurkeed suffered considerably from
> lack of fresh air during the run to Bombay.

Like the Captain in 'On the City Wall' who calls all natives
'niggers', both Pambé and Nurkeed appear to the 'kind gentle-

man' as 'benighted heathen', and he does not distinguish between them. He underestimates their drives and motivations as much as those who attribute to the Buria Kol 'a fantastic faith in wood-spirits, goblins of the rock and river-fiends', in 'The Judgment of Dungara' (*IBW*). In both instances the reality is more dangerous and sinister.

There are also, however, stories in which indigenous beliefs are accepted, and in which narrative power is derived from the inexplicable presence of the supernatural. The Indian servants in 'The Tomb of his Ancestors' (*TDW*), 'By Word of Mouth' and 'At the End of the Passage' are not surprised by supernatural manifestations and give imaginative expression to their acceptance of them. The vision of the memsahib in the blue gown in 'By Word of Mouth', the mysterious demon possession of 'At the End of the Passage' and the regiments' ghostly return in 'The Lost Legion' reveal the inadequacy of reason and common sense:

> 'But a dead Rissala,' said Halley, jerking his captive's wrists, – 'That is foolish talk, Kurruk Shah. The dead are dead' . . . 'The dead are dead, and for that reason they walk at night. What need to talk? We be men; we have our eyes and ears. Thou canst both see and hear them down the hillside,' said Kurruk Shah composedly.

Kipling seems to be most imaginatively engaged in those early stories which do not simply expose superstition, but blur the distinction between specious and genuine spirituality, or assert the psychological reality of a phenomenon. Narrative duplicities and conclusions which 'fail to satisfy' or fall short, embody the author's own uncertainty.

It is therefore important that *kismet* (destiny or fate) images the reluctance of some of the early stories to settle into probability and is explicitly linked with the action of the plot. 'But these things are *kismet*, and we only find out all about them just when any knowledge is too late', concludes the narrator at the end of 'Bitters Neat'; and in 'Watches of the Night' (*PTH*) the narrator urges us to 'Mark again how *kismet* works! . . . See once more the workings of *kismet*.' In each instance a single narrator begins as if in control of his material, but is soon displaced by another who takes over the narrative and offers a more complex and personal account, altering or amending what came before. The stories' endings, while supposedly explanatory, in fact make the situations that have been explored still more mysterious. As the speakers tease out the discrepancy between what is known and the possibility of complete knowledge, we become aware of a complex relationship between narrative and destiny.

Not surprisingly then, it is to Indian narratives, 'fairy tales' and 'Legends of Gods and Devils . . . learned in the servants' quarters', that Kipling turns for his early structural paradigms. In 'The Son of his Father', the child-protagonist privileges Eastern religious mythology over that of the West.

> Adam . . . revolted at the story of Genesis as untrue. A turtle, he said, upheld the world, and one half the adventures of Huzrut Nu [Father Noah] had never been told . . . Adam had heard of a saint who had made wooden cakes and pressed them to his stomach when he felt hungry, and the feeding of the multitude did not impress him. So it came about that a reading of miracles generally ended with discourses by Adam on other and much more astonishing miracles.[2]

What is interesting here is the treatment of the established Christian canon. The ironic play on the name 'Adam' and on the content of Genesis suggests that the traditional way of reading this material is inadequate. Indeed, Kipling seems to suggest that Christianity offers a set of stories that can be simplified and made into a pattern, but that the origins and causes of things are to be found in the proliferating narratives of Indian legend and fairy stories – even, paradoxically, those which remain untold.

In 'My Own True Ghost Story' (*PTH*), Kipling lists a number of superstitious beliefs:

> There are, in India, ghosts who take the form of fat, cold, pobby corpses, and hide in trees near the roadside till a traveller passes. Then they drop upon his neck and remain. There are also terrible ghosts of women who have died in childbed. These wander along the pathways at dusk, or hide

in the crops near a village and call seductively. But to answer
their call is death in this world and the next. Their feet are
turned backwards that all sober men may recognise them.
There are ghosts of little children who have been thrown into
wells. These haunt well-curbs and the fringes of jungles, and
wail under the stars, or catch women by the wrist and beg to
be taken up and carried.

This account is characterized by the pungency of the different
ghosts – each is a narrative gem and could be among the stories
that 'had never been told' above. In one sense this might be a list,
but on another level the narrative also reveals a personal preoccupation with the relationship between the supernatural and
the moral. Despite the ironic reference to 'sober men' and the
delicate suggestion of marginality in the locales ('trees near the
roadside', 'crops near a village', 'the fringes of the jungle'),
Kipling evidently expected moral responsibility even in things
beyond man's ken. Yet the difficulty, the complex and hazardous
moral choices, are written into the knife-edge alternation between
fantastic and real worlds until their inevitable fusion in the final
sentence. There is moral anxiety in the transference between the
spirit world and the world in which seductresses operate. Again
there is ultimately no separation: 'But to answer their call is death
in this world and the next.'
    Elsewhere in Kipling's Indian stories the paradigm of narrative
proliferation and the dialectic between the supernatural and the
moral, are represented in the iconography of the Great Wheel and
in the permutations of the Law. Here Kipling follows Sir Edwin
Arnold's *The Light of Asia* (a popular account of the life and
philosophy of the Buddha, known and loved by Kipling when he
was at school). Like Arnold, Kipling makes no distinction
between Dharma (Law) as 'the way things are' and Dharma as
'the Way' – a journey along an eightfold path to Nirvana (Salvation) through a cycle of existences (Arnold, 1870, pp. 109, 53).
For Kipling, then, the Law is both a rigid structure at the heart of
things and a spiritual quest. It is expressed in organic metaphors
and images of plants and animals: 'like a Giant Creeper that
dropped across everyone's back so that no one could escape', it

governs all events in the world, and must therefore be obeyed: 'Keep ye the Law, be swift in all obedience' (*JB*). But, at the same time, it figures as something beyond or outside these things. This is the 'miracle' apprehended by the eponymous Purun Bhagat at the moment of his death (*JB2*) and by the Lama in *Kim* at the end of his search for 'the Most Excellent Law': 'As a drop draws to water, so my soul drew near to the Great Soul which is beyond all things . . . By this time I knew the Soul had passed beyond the illusion of Time and Space and of Things. By this I knew I was free . . . Then my soul was all alone and I saw nothing.' Elsewhere in Kipling's writings, Samsara (the cyclical progress or stages of enlightenment or the cycle of births and deaths in worldly existence), is presented in the iconography of the Great Wheel. Rolling without intermission, the Wheel of Existence hurries men and gods 'from despair to despair' through suffering and death in innumerable incarnations. It is their actions, past and present, that determine how they rise and fall on the Wheel. As a result they can only display the kind of resig- nation displayed in 'At Twenty-Two' (*FSS*), for they live 'in bondage' to their own acts and can only hope 'to acquire Merit' and thereby ascent. At its most extreme the conception of the Wheel figures the possibility of a fall from human to animal status. So a cobra blocking the path in *Kim* prompts the Lama's comment: 'He is upon the Wheel as we are – a life ascending or descending – very far from deliverance. Great evil must the soul have done that is cast into this shape.' Kipling drew upon Arnold's descriptions in *Kim*, where the Great Wheel is presented with care and minute attention to detail:

Often the Lama made the living pictures the matter of his text, bidding Kim – too ready – note how the flesh takes a thousand thousand shapes, desirable or detestable as men reckon, but in truth of no account either way; and how the stupid spirit, bond-slave to the Hog, the Dove, and the Serpent – lusting after betel-nut, a new yoke of oxen, women, or the favour of kings – is bound to follow the body through all the Heavens and all the Hells, and strictly round again.

In many ways this passage can be seen as they key to Kipling's Indian stories, and indeed to many of his later writings. The cycle of transience is viewed not only as a metaphysic, but also as an aesthetic of fragmentation and renewal. The 'thousand thousand shapes' taken by the flesh generate as many 'living pictures', as many narratives. In the Wheel of Life Kipling found a metaphysic and an aesthetic that would acknowledge the reality of Love and Hate, and the reality of their co-existence.

Notes

1   This is an echo of the biblical phrase in Genesis 15.12. For Kipling's repeated reference to it see Kipling (1928, p. 19).
2   *To-day*, 1, 30 December 1893, p. 2. The Sussex Edition, *LST* p. 171, omits the last six lines of this paragraph.

2

'Just enough to tantalise':
Reincarnation, theosophy, the occult and metafiction

'There is always something alien about Kipling, as of a visitor from another planet', wrote T. S. Eliot (1941, p. 28). Even when Kipling left India in 1899, his writings continued to display an assertive and pragmatic public voice which confronts the surreal and the supernatural, and which is dependent upon a weight of unmentioned detail and event for its effect. A clue to the status of this voice may be found in a passage in the autobiography, which recounts the usurpation of the realities of war by a superior force. 'Here is a curious case', Kipling tells us:

> In the late summer, I think, of '13, I was invited to Ma-
> noeuvres round Frensham Ponds at Aldershot. The troop's
> were from the Eighth Division of the coming year –
> Guardsmen, Black Watch, and the rest, down to the horsed
> maxims – two per battalion. Many of the officers had been
> juniors in the Boer War, known to Gwynne, one of the guests,
> and some to me. When the sham fight was developing, the
> day turned blue-hazy, the sky lowered, and the heat struck
> like the Karroo, as one scuttled among the heaths, listening
> to the uncontrolled clang of the musketry fire. It came over
> me that anything might be afoot in such weather, pom-poms
> for instance, half heard on a flank, or the glint of a helio
> through a cloud-drift. In short I conceived the whole pressure
> of our dead of the Boer War flickering and re-forming as the
> horizon flickered in the heat; the galloping feet of a single
> horse, and a voice once well-known that passed chanting

ribaldry along the flank of a crack battalion. ('But Winnie is
one of the lost – poor dear!' was that song, if any remember
it or its singer in 1900–1901.) In an interval, while we lay
on the grass, I told Gwynne what was in my head; and some
officers also listened. The finale was to be manoeuvres abandoned and a hurried calling-off of all arms by badly fright-
ened Commandants – the men themselves sweating with
terror though they knew not why. (1937, p. 214)

The unaccountable fear expressed at the end of this extract
points to other kinds of narrative discourse concealed within
Kipling's stories. Signalled by images of the blinded and the
blindfold, these concern imaginative vision, modes of perception
in which artistic inspiration and writing become metaphors for
terrifying and unknown ways of seeing. Here, as in the stories
considered in the first chapter, such modes of perception are
related to the spiritual and the magical. In 'The Finest Story in
the World' (*MI*), 'Wireless' (*TD*) and 'They' (*TD*), the overt
obsession with the technicalities of ancient history, wireless telegraphy and motor cars masks metafictional investigations of the
ambiguities of authorship and of the morality of art. In these
stories, the ghost or dream text is again associated with what
Gosse calls 'feminine' modes – these are subversive, repressed
and represented within the aesthetic as a fragmentary and (sometimes) poetic force.[1] The power of inner vision is unobtrusively
given to women or to unheroic figures; and the conflicting voices,
multiple perspectives, repetitions, forgettings, intersections of the
real and the imagined, the physical and the emotional, are also
closely associated with the child.

In *Something of Myself* Kipling claimed that he started to write,
but never completed, the story that he had conceived at Frensham:
'The notion so obsessed me that I wrote out the beginning at once.
But in cold blood it seemed more and more fantastic and absurd,
unnecessary and hysterical' (p. 215). However, problematic fantasy and hallucinatory vision underlie the most brusquely 'masculine' of Kipling's writings, and the qualities of the 'fantastic and
absurd, unnecessary and hysterical' are integral to his narrative
registers. The thematic and structural mingling of literal and

figurative, public and private, is acted out in the play of Kipling's metaphors. As T. E. Apter points out:

> The fantasist's metaphors combine the conflation of vehicle and tenor with strange and new associations; figurative language becomes the only means of making literal assertions, for ordinary meanings fragment, expand, splinter, either because some new, unknown order prevails, or because the former order functions haphazardly or piecemeal. Thus the fantasist must piece together a new language. (1982, p. 3)

Kipling made a 'new language' out of scientific advance. The use of early cinema to image the *unheimlich*[2] in 'Mrs Bathurst' (*TD*) fulfils Apter's notion of figurative language as something that, in an instance where there is no route back to the original grounds of comparison, may exceed the conventionally metaphoric. In this story Pyecroft concedes that 'seein' ' and 'hearin' ' do not always correspond with 'what transpired'. Perhaps the most striking metaphor employed by Kipling in this respect is that of reincarnation.

Reincarnation was a common theme in popular fiction from the mid-century onwards, but Kipling's use of it in his stories transcended conventional limits. While others use it to embroider popular romance, or to bring historical narrative to life, Kipling draws a rich imaginative analogy between reincarnation and the mystery of poetic inspiration. The analogy is used to convey a clearer sense of the nature of imagination. Yet the special aptness of the analogy is that a total revelation of the sources of imagination must remain permanently elusive. Like the narrator of 'Wireless', the reader witnesses 'just enough to tantalise'.

Kipling would have first encountered the notion of reincarnation in the 'stories and Indian nursery songs all unforgotten' of his childhood. In Kipling's fictional account of his childhood at Lorne Lodge, Punch reads Rhoda Broughton's *Cometh Up as a Flower* (1867). Broughton's novel reflects a widespread contemporary interest in reincarnation that derived from the infiltration into the West of Eastern thought, particularly Buddhism, from the 1850s onwards.[3] Kipling would have been early acquainted

with at least two other versions of reincarnation: that contained in
The Jatakas (first translated into English by T. W. Rhys Davids in
1880), and that recounted in Sir Edwin Arnold's *The Light of Asia*
(1870).

The Jatakas are moral fables deriving from the sixth century
which purport to tell of the wise actions of the Buddha in previous
incarnations. Kipling's father shows his acquaintance with them
in *Beast and Man in India* (1891), and they were among the source
material for Kipling's *Jungle Books*, *Just So Stories* and *Kim*. In
Something of Myself Kipling remembers writing 'a half-chapter of
the Lama sitting down in the blue-green shadows at the foot of a
glacier, telling Kim stories out of the Jatakas, which was truly
beautiful' (1937, p. 141). Ultimately he regarded the section as
'otiose' and removed it, but he refers twice in the novel to the
twenty-seventh Jataka, 'Abhina Jataka' – 'The Story of Con-
stancy' (Rhys Davids, 1880, vol. 1, p. 263). On each occasion the
Lama tells the story of the fettered elephant to illustrate the idea of
reincarnation:

> Further testimony is not needed . . . Thou wast sent for an
> aid. That aid removed, my search came to naught. Therefore
> we will go out again together, and our search is sure . . . I
> acquired merit when I sent thee to the Gates of Learning,
> and gave thee the jewel that is wisdom. Thou didst return, I
> saw even now, a follower of Sakamuni, the Physician, whose
> altars are many in Bhotiyal. It is sufficient. We are together,
> and all things are as they were.

Again, when Kim expresses surprise at the timeless quality of
their relationship – 'It is less than three days since we took road
together, and it is as though it were a hundred years' – the
Lama's reply is founded upon this belief. 'Perhaps in a former life
it was permitted that I should have rendered thee some service
. . . I freed thee from a trap; or having caught thee on a hook in
the days when I was not enlightened, cast thee back into the
river.' Later the Lama claims that 'The Keeper of the Images in
the Wonder House was in past life a very wise Abbot', and, with
delicious irony, that the troublesome old Hindu lady had 'many,
many millions of lives before her'.

Reincarnation is a central theme in *Kim*, but unlike many of his contemporaries, Kipling resisted the temptation to use it for a love story, and this provoked criticism. As a reviewer for the *New York Critic* wrote in 1901: 'We are willing to let Mr Kipling treat the love-interest as a negligible quality in fiction, but then we must have the true romance in some other adequate form' (vol. 39, p. 466); or, in the words of the *Independent*: 'The complete absence of female influence from *Kim* will seem to some a masculine attraction more effective for its rarity' (vol. 53, p. 2415). Throughout Kipling's work, from the memsahib in the blue gown of 'By Word of Mouth' to the reappearance of Aunty Armine in 'A Madonna of the Trenches', we are given tantalizingly brief glimpses of death-defying love. But he reserved reincarnation for carefully considered thematic purposes of his own.

'What rot it all is!' remarks Charlie in 'The Finest Story in the World'. He is referring to Mortimer Collins's *Transmigration* (1874), a story of reincarnated love in three volumes. There is indeed little to recommend Collins's narrative, but the structure of Edwin Arnold's *The Wonderful Adventures of Phra the Phoenician* (1890), not mentioned by Charlie, is strikingly similar to Kipling's first fictional presentation of the theme of reincarnation in 'The Finest Story in the World'. *Phra* follows the incarnations of a young Phoenician merchant from British slave-consort to a Druid wife, to a Roman centurion, a supporter of King Harold, a Saxon thane, and a young man in the reign of Queen Elizabeth. He preserves his identity throughout, and is accompanied by the spirit of his first love, Blowden, in the shape of 'sweet ambassadors forever crossing my path', until their final transfiguration at the end.

In 'The Finest Story in the World', the nineteenth-century bank clerk Charlie also remembers former lives – in his case Greek and Norse 'riot, piracy and death in unnamed seas'. But Kipling subverts Arnold's theme in *Phra*, making Charlie's revelations confused – 'a maddening jumble' – and elusive: 'The Fates are so careful to shut the doors'. And rather than foregrounding romance, we are told that: 'the love of woman . . . kills remembrance'. Instead Kipling uses Charlie's fragmentary narrative of 'Half a dozen and several and separate existences' to explore the

notion of imagination as 'imperfect memory' and to write with
accuracy and conviction of the unknown. 'I [was] amazed . . . at
the tone of command in which it was flung out,' the narrator says.
As the story proceeds, it reveals an investigation of the nature
of the self seen in terms of reincarnation, and an interest in the
relationship between writing and 'truth'. In doing so it explores
the ambiguities of 'the author', for Charlie as author does not
know either himself or the value of the work that is produced by
'himself' in another form. 'It came by itself', he says. Kipling
seems to suggest that the author is in one sense the unconscious,
embodied in the Greek slave or Viking seaman. The unconscious
is here plural, unknown to itself even as it is manifested in
language. 'I looked at him, wondering whether it were possible
that he did not know the originality, the power of the notion that
had come his way', muses the narrator.

The nature and details of the narrative are further complicated
by the doubling of story-tellers – the fact that the actual narrator
is someone who is trying to write down 'Charlie's' story. Charlie
is unable to write his story, he can only speak it. But because the
narrator confuses the notion of truth with Charlie's words, he too
never achieves a complete transcription of the story:

> Only let me know, let me write, the story with sure knowl-
> edge that I wrote the truth, and I would burn the manuscript
> as a solemn sacrifice. Five minutes after the last line was
> written I would destroy it all. But I must be allowed to write
> it with absolute certainty.

Ironically, the narrative plays on words like 'truth' and 'reality'
to suggest that language is not to be grasped as something that
simply mirrors experience or the world. 'It's only a notion, but
sometimes it seems just as real as if it was true', Charlie says.
Instead the narrative implies that language and 'art' can only
present their own experience, which does not refer to the world.
So, in Kipling's writings, detail does not necessarily produce
meaning. Rather, as John Bayley points out, the stories create
a 'false structure': 'The antics of display are . . . [a] form of
reticence . . . The more "authentic" the narrator . . . the more
marked the unreality' (1986, p. 27).

The negative role of love in 'The Finest Story in the World' endorses this hint of the unsaid and is also fascinating because it is so enigmatic. As we have seen, Kipling implies that love closes the door on remembrance, and that forgetting is an essential part of reincarnation. In this story women are seen as seductresses who, through the power of their love, draw men into the illusory world of existence: 'They kiss you behind closed doors.' There is a close relationship here between Charlie's mother and his girl-friend. Charlie imagines that he is rejecting his mother for the girl, but the narrative suggests that both women are part of a pattern of life and death in which the woman as perceived by the man becomes 'She'. Here transience is seen as part of a larger pattern of renewal. It is time's boldness and blindness that creates the enigma. Just as the works of the 'soul' which endure are perfected in the cycle of reincarnation, the new work of art depends on the death of the old form which, paradoxically, makes the repetition possible. The cycle of life and death, bound upon the Great Wheel, depends upon repetitions and forgettings which can never be known:

> Charlie spoke on and on, and on; while I, separated from him by thousands of years, was considering the beginnings of things. Now I understood why the Lords of Life and Death shut the doors so carefully behind us. It is that we may not remember our first and most beautiful wooings. Were this not so, our world would be without inhabitants in a hundred years.

Kipling's use of reincarnation to explore deeply felt metaphysical convictions of his own is also evident in 'Wireless', where, as J. M. S. Tompkins suggests, 'the ingenious parallels . . . run out in mystery' (1959, p. 219). 'For reasons of my own', the narrator tells us, 'I was deeply interested in Marconi experiments at their outset in England'; and the action of 'Wireless' takes place in a chemist's shop where an early wireless experiment is underway.[4] The pharmacist's nephew tunes the receiving set to pick up signals in Morse code from Poole, but the radio messages coincide with a supernatural transmission at the front of the shop. The narrator's interest is intensified as Mr Shaynor, the tubercular pharmacist's assistant and lover of 'Fanny Brand', locks onto the wavelengths of the Keatsian 'daemon' and writes a tawdry version of 'The Eve of St Agnes', contaminated by other of Keats's poems.

By establishing that Shaynor has never read Keats's poetry, but that his experiences are not unlike those of Keats, Kipling uses the early experiments with wireless telegraphy to conceive the recondite nature of poetic inspiration. As Gilbert points out, in this sense the poet is seen as the receiving set tuned by experience to a corresponding wavelength, and the inspiration consists of radio waves searching for an instrument that will translate the weak broadcast signals (1972, pp. 165–6). But the narrative also explores the nature of poetic imagination in terms of the distinction between Keats as a poet, and 'Keats' as a metonym for his poems. Mr Shaynor, the reincarnation of the 'author', is here being possessed by the language of Keats's poetry. What he experiences is a repetition of Keats's original and painful creation of 'The Eve of St Agnes', but the agonizing creation of something new is now seen as the discovery of something already written.

> 'Not yet – not yet,' he muttered. 'Wait a minute. *Please* wait a minute. I shall get it then –
>
> > Our magic windows fronting on the sea ,
> > The dangerous foam of desolate seas . . .
> > For aye.
>
> *Ouh*, my God!'
> From head to heel he shook – shook from the marrow of his bones outwards – then leaped to his feet with raised arms, and slid the chair screeching across the tiled floor where it struck the drawers behind and fell with a jar. Mechanically, I stooped to recover it.

The few lines of 'clear vision' or 'pure magic' have already been written, but that writing is more than writing. The 'blindfold soul' which Keats and Mr Shaynor share within the Wheel of Life exists in the unconscious and in language. Indeed, writing becomes a metaphor for preternatural ways of seeing, which is what Keats imagines in his own lines:

Charmed magic casements, opening on the foam
Of perilous seas, in faery lands forlorn.

On another level, the panic explored in the story is also associated with the fear of 'seeing', which is explained in terms of
conscious and unconscious divisions within the self. What is
significant here is the distinction implicitly drawn between two
experiences of panic. 'The unknown Power kicking and fighting
to get loose' that possesses Shaynor mediates between reincarnation and visitations of an alien spirit. Mr Shaynor experiences
the unconscious fear that is involved in possession by 'another'.
This is the vision embodied in Keats's language. By contrast,
however, the narrator consciously experiences a terrifying and
unexplained division within himself. This is presented as a fear of
acknowledging what he has intuitively understood:

> As dreamers accept and explain the upheaval of landscapes
> and the resurrection of the dead, with excerpts from the
> evening hymn or the multiplication table, so I had accepted
> the facts, whatever they might be, that I should witness, and
> had devised a theory, sane and plausible to my mind, that
> explained them all. Nay, I was even in advance of my facts,
> walking hurriedly before them, assured that they would fit
> my theory.

In *Something of Myself* Kipling's description of himself as totally in
the possession or thrall of his 'daemon' is unqualified.[5] By contrast, this division between an innate scepticism and a deeply felt
imaginative conviction in 'Wireless' has a compelling psychological and aesthetic power, and remains a leitmotif throughout
Kipling's work.

In the final analysis, a large part of the fascination of 'Wireless'
derives precisely from the impossibility of distinguishing the
author's sleight of hand from the separate discourses which consti-
tute the narrative. The narrator 'bewildered among the batteries
and rods', is giving nothing away. And it is difficult to tell how
seriously Kipling takes his own story. Like the electric current
generated by the radio transmission, the details of the story
'cohere' only as long as the reader is actually engaged in reading

it. The garish lights flickering over the contents of the chemist's shop – 'glass jars – red, green, and blue . . . orris, Kodak films, vulcanite, tooth-powder, sachets and almond cream' – and the recurrent image of the corsetted woman on the 'gold-framed toilet water advertisement' suggest other stories, which remain untold; and the mingling of 'spiritual' with wireless telegraphy undermines the seemingly serious nature of the psychical quest. The use of telegraphy as a parodic trope is particularly evident in Shaynor's nephew's final remarks.

> 'Their transmitters are all right, but their receivers are out of order, so they only get a dot here and a dash there. Nothing clear.'
> 'Why is that?'
> 'God knows – and Science will know to-morrow. Perhaps the induction is faulty; perhaps the receivers aren't tuned to receive just the number of vibrations per second that the transmitter sends. Only a word here and there. Just enough to tantalise.'

In 'Wireless', as in 'The Finest Story in the World', the reader is left at the end with unanswered questions and with a sense of the partial revelation of mystery. In both stories, and in later stories (for example, 'On the Gate' (*DC*) and 'Uncovenanted Mercies' (*LR*), where souls are rehabilitated for future use, Kipling's treatment of reincarnation is characterized by uncertainty. The imaginative analogy between reincarnation and modern scientific discovery enhances the excitement of a revelation always imminent but never ultimately attained. And if, as David Trotter points out, the conflicting voices are not explained away as 'paradox' or 'enigma', but seen at work in the production of story or poem or attitude, subtle and radical intimations emerge (1984, p. 667). To select the parts that seem to make logical sense is to produce an 'identikit' Kipling, or an ideological artefact, and the complexities are lost. In some ways the narrative voices represent the negation or repudiation of personality: from the outset of his career Kipling explores their creative potential.

The creative value of the thin dividing-line between Kipling's assents and dissents, his loves and hates, is also evident in his response to theosophy. The treatment of theosophy in 'The Sending of Dana Da' (*IBW*) again demonstrates his ability to derive special narrative power by playing off parody against unquestioning belief, knowledge against naivete. The pun on 'sending' (sending-up) in the story's title hints that the narrative will not prove as straightforward as it might at first appear. Like 'The Finest Story in the World' and 'Wireless', 'The Sending of Dana Da' challenges narrative convention. As ordinary meanings are suspended, the familiar takes on strange and unstable forms, showing up gaps in perception and revealing new associations and patterns whose presence had not been suspected.

Theosophy, or its Sanskrit equivalent 'Brahma-Vidya', means 'God-knowledge'.[6] Both ancient and modern theosophical creeds proclaim the possibility of the direct experience of God by man. This is the 'inner' spirit of all religions as opposed to their 'outer' dogma, rites and ceremonies. Theosophy also denotes a body of information concerning God, man and the universe ('Divine Wisdom'), handed down by a long succession of prophets, teachers and writers. Its texts include the Hindu Upanishads, Chinese Taoism, the Egyptian Book of the Dead and the Hebrew Kabbala.

The 'Modern Theosophical Society' was founded by Helena Petrovna Blavatsky and Henry Steele Olcott in New York in November 1875. It claimed to be a modern expression of the Upanishadic 'Brahma-Vidya', and set out to explain 'the origin of the world and of man and the ultimate destinies of our race . . . the nature of other worlds and states of existence differing from those of our present life' (Sinnett, 1883, pp. v–vi). Between 1878 and 1880 the Modern Theosophical Society was briefly affiliated with the Hindu Arya Samaj, but there was a parting of the ways after Madame Blavatsky's conversion to Buddhism in 1880.

For the most part, however, the Society's supporters were less impressed by Madame Blavatsky's highly idiosyncratic interpretation – 'Religio-Philosophico-Cosmico-Ethico' – of a heterogeneous body of Sanskrit texts than by the demonstrations of her remarkable psychic powers and the fascination of her personality (Blavatsky, 1889, p. xiii). Yeats called her 'a great passionate nature, a sort of female Dr Johnson'. Even when her activities were discredited by the Society for Psychical Research in 1885, its investigators were obliged to conclude: 'We think she has achieved a title to permanent remembrance as one of the most accomplished, ingenious, and interesting imposters of history' (Leonard, 1976, p. 103).

By an interesting coincidence, in 1882, when Kipling left school to take up a post on the *Civil and Military Gazette*, A. P. Sinnett, editor of its sister-paper, the *Pioneer*, had become 'a devout believer' and was using the newspapers for 'propaganda'. Simla, where Kipling spent his leaves, was 'Full of the aftermaths of Theosophy as taught by Madame Blavatsky. My father knew the lady . . . I was not so fortunate, but came across queer, bewildered, old people, who lived in an atmosphere of "manifestations" running about their houses' (1937, p. 58).

During the course of two visits to Simla, Madame Blavatsky had made converts by demonstrating her ability to produce 'precipitated letters' (letters conveyed by psychic currents) and her mastery of 'psychological telegraphy' (instantaneous communication with secret initiates in Tibet). Most notable, however, was the manifestation of a teacup when an extra guest arrived unexpectedly at a tea-party in the Himalayas. Having by these means secured the conversion of Sinnett, she lost no time putting him in touch with Koot-Hoomi-Lal-Singh, one of the Tibetan brotherhood whom she believed to be in possession of the secret doctrine. Sinnett received instruction from the adept by means of precipitated letters, but, as sceptics were quick to point out, was himself obliged to correspond in the normal manner. At a later date, he received a 'precipitated portrait profile' of the master (Macdonald, 1885, p. 711). Sinnett eventually resigned his editorship of the *Pioneer* and became the chief spokesman of theosophy in the West.

In *Something of Myself*, Kipling described his anger at the foolishness of the newly converted editor 'which got on the nerves not only of the public, but of a proof-reader, who at the last moment salted an impassioned leader on the subject with, in brackets: *'What do you bet this is a dam' lie?'* (p. 58). He also makes ironic reference to theosophy in *Letters of Marque* where he describes meeting a 'hard-headed Scotch merchant with a taste for Spiritualism who begged me to tell him whether there was really anything in Theosophy and whether Tibet was full of levitating *chelas* as he believed'. Kipling's own response to theosophy is reflected in 'The Sending of Dana Da', where a Theosophical Lodge is devastated by the inexplicable presence of materialized kittens. The miraculous 'Sending' is, in fact, no more than the judicious placing of the kittens by a heavily bribed servant ('Very few kittens now in the bazaar. Ask Lone Sahib's sweeper's wife').

'The Sending of Dana Da' is clearly a satire on the dissemination of theosophy in Simla. 'Once upon a time, some people in India made a new Heaven and a new Earth out of broken tea-cups, a missing brooch or two, and a hairbrush. These were hidden under bushes, or stuffed into holes in the hillside.' Ironic references to 'the Simla Creed', 'the Tea-Cut Creed' and 'crockery' throughout the story recall the process of Sinnett's conversion, as does the nature of the manifestations: 'letters dropped from the ceiling unstamped'; 'unseen hands played Gluck and Beethoven on finger-bowls'. At the end of the story, the appeal to 'Thoth-Ra-Tum-Sennacherib', the 'authorised head' of the Creed, recalls Koot-Hoomi-Lal-Singh, the adept with whom Sinnett supposedly studied.

Throughout 'The Sending of Dana Da' Kipling mocks the eclectic and esoteric nature of the Creed. He cites borrowings from Freemasonry, Rosicrucianism, Egyptian philosophy, the Vedas, the Zend-Aresta, white and black magic and voodoo, and lists their symbols: 'pentacles . . . *crux ansata* . . . *swastikas* . . . Triple Tau . . . curses from the Rites of Mizraim and Memphis and the Commination of Jugana'. 'This religion was too elastic for ordinary use', he concludes. He also parodies the credulity of its adherents: 'people so absolutely free from superstition that they ascribed anything a little out of the common to the Agencies'. Happy to pay large subscriptions in anticipation of the *frisson*, they are also particularly excited by the possibility of a schism: 'seeing that an outsider who had been working on independent lines could create kittens, whereas their own rulers had never gone beyond crockery'.

Yet elsewhere in his writings, and in stories written at the same time as this one, Kipling delights in psychic phenomena, esoteric and secret doctrine, and the pleasure of initiation. We have

already seen his description of Strickland in 'Miss Youghal's Sais'
in chapter 1. In 'Beyond the Pale', there is another such initiate
whom the narrator celebrates: 'Trejago knew far too much about
these things, as I have said. No Englishman should be able to
translate object-letters. But Trejago spread all the trifles on the lid
of his office-box and began to puzzle them out.' This kind of
knowledge is also reflected in Kipling's treatment of Freemasonry.
Elsewhere the cult of the insider is translated into the secret skills
of crafts, trades and professions, and accounts for a 'knowingness'
in the manner of these stories. Despite the mockery, even in 'The
Sending of Dana Da', it is clear that the narrator loves to be on
the 'inside' himself. He is condescending towards Dana Da's
transcription of the words of the 'manifestation' and assumes a
superior arcane knowledge. He claims, for example, that they
'would have adopted Voodoo and Obeah had it known anything
about them'; and that 'They did not call it a Sending . . . Icelandic
magic was not in their programme'. The narrator's long and
gratuitous digression on the origin of Dana Da's name is itself
instinct with scholarly mystification:

> Now setting aside Dana of the *New York Sun*, Dana is a Bhil
> name, and Da fits no native of India unless you accept the
> Bengali De as the original spelling. Da is Lap or Finnish;
> and Dana Da was neither Finn, Chin, Bhil, Bengali, Lap,
> Nair, Gond, Romany, Magh, Bokhariot, Kurd, Armenian,
> Levantine, Jew, Persian, Punjabi, Madrasi, Parsee, nor
> anything else known to ethnologists.

The reader's growing feeling that the narrator's attitude is
harder to place than at first appears is confirmed by contrasting
styles and tones within the narrative. On the one hand, there is
ironic play on the scientific vocabulary of the Society for Psychical
Research. At the beginning of the story Dana Da describes
himself as an 'Independent Experimenter'; in recounting his
'Manifestations', Lone Sahib notes 'hour and minute, as every
Psychical Observer is bound to do', and, tongue in cheek, the
narrator himself concludes: 'The letter proved conclusively that
there had been a hitch in the Psychic Current which, colliding
with a Dual Identity, had interfered with the Percipient Activity

all along the main line.' On the other hand, this language is set against the 'terminology of the Creed', which is 'deeply mysterious', and allows for a number of entirely subjective interpretations: 'Lone Sahib read the letter in five different fashions and was beginning a sixth.' Here, the narrative implies that how you read is dependent on whether you are a believer or not, for the theosophists are tacitly aware of their participation in a game:

> An outsider would have translated all the tangle thus: 'Look out! You laughed at me once, and now I am going to make you sit up.'
> Lone Sahib's co-religionists found that meaning in it; but their translation was refined and full of four-syllable words.

It is equally the case that you can endow words with meaning if you so choose. 'These words may not be quite correct, but they accurately express the sense of the house', the narrator claims elsewhere. Hence 'sense' is dependent on subjective interpretation. And throughout the story, the reader is also engaged in unravelling meaning. Consider, for example, the following paragraph:

> Now a Sending is a horrible arrangement, first invented, they say, in Iceland. It is a Thing sent by a wizard, and may take any form, but, most generally, wanders about the land in the shape of a little purple cloud till it finds the Sendee, and him it kills by changing into the form of a horse, or a cat, or a man without a face. It is not strictly a native patent, though *chamars* of the skin and hide castes can, if irritated, despatch a Sending which sits on the breast of their enemy by night and nearly kills him. Very few natives care to irritate *chamars* for this reason.

Do the fairy-tale language and light-hearted mockery of the first two sentences modulate in mid-paragraph with the words 'or a man without a face', a condition of fear and anxiety which recalls the warning contained in the story's epigraph: ' "When the Devil rides on your chest remember the *chamar*" – Native Proverb'? Or does the tone remain consistent throughout?

In 'The Sending of Dana Da', as in 'In the House of Suddhoo',

'The magic that is always demanding gifts is not true magic.' But in both stories the exposure of trickery is inseparable from a strong suggestion of uncanny power. Indeed, in 'The Sending of Dana Da', when the narrator says that 'the mere words on paper were creepy and uncanny to behold', it is not easy to dismiss his fears.

The equivocation in Kipling's response to the psychic and the supernatural remains characteristic. The conflicting voices in his stories combine to create an uncertainty which also derives from the fact that the narrator's and the reader's imaginative and emotional responses are constantly being surprised and extended. 'Well, I don't know how it *looks* like, but let be how 'twill', says Jabez to Jesse in 'Friendly Brook' (*ADC*). The evasiveness and reticence of their dialogue is entirely characteristic:

> 'What did he say when you told him that?' Jabez demanded, with a little change of voice.
> 'Why? What did he say to you when *you* told him?' was the answer.
> 'What he said to you, I reckon, Jesse.'
> 'Then you don't need me to say it over agin, Jabez.'
> 'Well, let be how 'twill, what was he gettin' *after* when he said what he said to me?' Jabez insisted.
> '*I* dunno; unless you tell me what manner o' words he said to *you*.'

Nowhere is this uncertainty more subtly explored than in 'They', which records the perceptions and feelings of a figure moving through a space that is both real and imagined. Elements of the narrative are concretely realized even though it is at times uncertain whether the narrator is dreaming or actually perceiving an external reality. Narrator, blind woman and child join forces in this story to crystallize the powers of selfhood and of narrative investigated in 'The Sending of Dana Da', 'The Finest Story in the World' and 'Wireless'.

In 'They' a bereaved father pays three visits to a mysterious country house inhabited by a blind woman and filled with the laughter of unseen children. The fairy-tale description of the first visit, in which the narrator, deeply moved, feels as if he is in an enchanted land, contrasts sharply with the second, in which a desperate search for a doctor and nurse to attend a dying child in a nearby village forces the narrative to engage with harsh reality. During his third and final visit the narrator perceives the significance of his compulsion to come: a kiss imprinted on the palm of his upturned hand reveals the proximity of his dead child; he now comprehends that 'They' are spirits, and not living children, and with this recognition comes the bitter knowledge that he can never return.

At the opening of the story the psychic is presented partly in terms of the psychological need of the narrator. When he retraces his journey on a map he realizes that the House Beautiful does not exist. If he seems to half-create this mysterious house to which he is so compulsively drawn, the power of subconscious motivation could also account for the ambiguous presence of the hidden children: '"How many are they!", I said . . . Her forehead puckered a little in thought. "I don't quite know," she said simply. "Sometimes more – sometimes less."' Throughout, the reservations of the blind woman and her constant demands for reassurance reflect a similar ambivalence. Together they explore the uncertain 'rights' of emotional experience:

'They came because I loved them – because I needed them.
I – I must have made them come. Was that wrong, think
you? . . . They were not mine by right . . . *not* for me!'

'It isn't foolish, do you think? . . . you – you aren't laughing
at me? . . . You think it is wrong then?'

But this tentativeness and uncertainty conflict with an extraordinary intensity of feeling and utter conviction in the telling of the tale. 'I saw a couple up at the window now, and I think I heard a little chap in the grounds', reports the narrator during his first visit. Throughout the story his detailed portrayal of the children and their toys and nurseries is in keeping with the servants' unquestioning belief in the children's reality. The butler, Madden, is solicitous for the welfare of 'our young gentleman in blue'. And Jenny, walking in the woods with her child, says 'placidly' to the narrator, 'You'll find yours indoors, I reckon'. The full realization that 'They' are ghosts comes only at the very end, in the ironic description of the despicable Mr Turpin's terror: 'His eyes rolled into every corner of the room wide with horror. He half opened the door through which he had entered, but I noticed it shut again – from without and firmly.' This is followed almost immediately by the extraordinary physical intensity of the kiss, which represents the most complete of the intersections, throughout the story, of the real and the imagined, the phsyical and the emotional:

> I ceased to tap the leather – was, indeed, calculating the cost of the shed – when I felt my relaxed hand taken and turned softly between the soft hands of a child. So at last I had triumphed. In a moment I would turn and acquaint myself with those quickfooted wanderers.
>
> The little brushing kiss fell in the centre of my palm – as a gift on which the fingers were, once, expected to close: as the all-faithful half-reproachful signal of a waiting child not used to neglect even when grown-ups were busiest – a fragment of the mute code devised very long ago.
>
> Then I knew. And it was as if I had known from the first day when I looked across the lawn at the high window.

Here the nature of the child is explored in terms of the narrator's hopes and ambitions, feelings and desires, even perhaps his guilt. His commentary does not so much explain as replicate within itself the hesitancy of his responses. Both the complex time-sequence, and the movement of the paragraph through simile, register growing awareness, changes of feeling and momentary perceptions that cannot be resolved into a consistent view or attitude or belief: retraversing uncertainties, rather than resolving them. For the child is inexplicably and palpably *present*, yet, paradoxically, as the narrator recognizes, her absence is equally essential to him. Held within and without, she is a powerful daemonic figure: the creative impulse for the story itself.

The nature of perception not based in the eye is further explored through the character of the Blind Woman, who leads a full, if involuntary, psychic life. The narrator witnesses her innate ability to see the 'Colours', bodies of psychic energy emanating from the personality whose limits extend beyond the physical body and reveal its essence. She also traces the contours of the 'Egg', which represents the universe – macrocosm of the physical body – closed in a single shell.[7]

According to Victorian hypotheses the 'Colours' were believed to be the medium of thought vibrations and acts of magic. In *The Mysterious Universe*, James Jeans's description of the 'Astral Light' resembled what Jung was later to call the 'Collective Unconscious': 'Every thought that we think stamps an indelible impression on the impressionable surface of that plane . . . and then passes away from our immediate control into the pulsating ocean of vitality and feeling to influence other minds for good or for ill' (Regardie, 1932, p. 69). Such theories accord with Kipling's belief that artistic inspiration is 'given', and Kipling's treatment of them in 'They' explores further the idea in 'The Sending of Dana Da', 'The Finest Story in the World' and 'Wireless' that writing is a kind of occult experience. 'The magic of literature lies in the words, and not in any man', Kipling told an audience at the Royal Academy in May 1906, rephrasing a rather coy fictional statement made fifteen years previously in *The Light that Failed*. 'Don't you understand, darling', says Dick to Maisie:

> Good work has nothing to do with – doesn't belong to – the person who does it. It's put into him or her from the outside. . . . All we can do is learn how to do our work, to be masters of our materials instead of servants, and never to be afraid of anything.

In 'They', the narrator's fascination with the arcane, and the disproportionate yet cryptic references to it in the story, reflects a continuing preoccupation with the similarities between the writer, the mystic and the psychic: in different ways they each seek to understand and identify themselves with the hidden powers of the psyche.

The ending of 'They' relates these insights to those problems of narrative which involve the expectation of completion, the final revelation of mystery and some kind of 'discovery' or emotional growth or development. According to this convention, the kiss in 'They' would represent the powerful and definitive 'resolution', but the fact that the moment of insight is also tentative and teasing, and held within uncertainties only partially resolved, testifies to an important narrative complexity. During the course of the story the reader becomes accustomed to the curious mixture of certainty and ambivalence in the narrative, and does not register the strangeness of it: the kiss emphasizes the uncertainty, rather than resolving it as the narrator seems to think. 'Then I knew', the narrator says, and at this moment the reader also perceives ambiguities that have passed unnoticed earlier in the story. 'We are so out of the world', the Blind Woman says, and the narrator refers to being 'quite the other side of the country', and 'clean out of my known marks'. The final encounter takes place in twilight and is epitomized in the shadowy game of hide-and-seek:

> There were bolt-holes innumerable – recesses in walls, em-brasures of deep-slitten windows now darkened, whence they could start up behind us; and abandoned fireplaces, six feet deep in the masonry, as well as the tangle of communi-cating doors. Above all, they had the twilight for their helper in the game.

But it is also the case that the moment of insight is extended throughout the suspended time and space of the narrative, for 'the tremendous secret', the thing 'hidden' and 'miraculous' is known to the majority of the characters. 'Mrs Madden . . . she saw . . . And Knew, Hers', the Blind Woman tells the narrator. This goes for Jenny too. Even the narrator possesses 'knowledge' that is simultaneous with the events as they are told: his final 'triumph' is accomplished by means of 'a fragment of the mute code devised very long ago'. This is a brilliant narrative stroke.

But unlike the inhabitants of the House Beautiful and the nearby village, the narrator finds that this kind of knowledge is intimately associated with loss. Part of the story's poignancy derives from his intuitive sense of prohibition and his conviction that it is to the world of the living that he must return. 'For me it would be wrong', he tells the Blind Woman, 'For me only'. The image of the screen separating the living and the dead confirms the narrator's earlier perception of himself as 'a trespasser', 'astray', and it is Madden's awareness of this that explains his puzzling conversation with the narrator earlier in the story:

'Have you seen 'em again, Sir – this morning?'
'Yes, but they're well broke to cars. I couldn't get any of them within twenty yards of it.'
He looked at me carefully as a scout considers a stranger – not as a menial should lift his eyes to a divinely appointed superior.
'I wonder why,' he said just above the breath that he drew.

The narrator 'finds' the children only when he stops looking for them. The invisible taboo is symbolized by the framing figure of the yew horseman with levelled spear (double symbol of death) mentioned at the beginning, middle and end of the story: 'Here, then, I stayed; a horseman's green spear laid at my breast; held by the exceeding beauty of that jewel in that setting.'

Notes

1 See Introduction p. 2.
2 For the uncanny see Freud (1919, pp. 212–52).
3 Scholarly works by V. Fausboll, Max Muller and T. W. Rhys Davids, and popular works by Sir Edwin Arnold, Bishop Bigander and A. P. Sinnett reflected this interest. With the founding of the English Society for Psychical Research in 1882, the concept of reincarnation also played its part in the growing interest in psychical research of the period. See Humphreys (1968); Sangharakshita (1956); Babbitt (1931); Macdonald (1885); George (1913).
4 Oliver Lodge conducted the world's first public demonstration of wireless telegraphy. The discovery of radio waves (1888), X-rays (1895), and radioactivity (1896) confronted scientists with phenomena they could not explain in conventional terms. To Balfour, Lodge and William Crookes, the existence of radio waves suggested that mental telepathy, extrasensory perception and clairvoyance, were at least worthy of investigation. See *Proceedings of the Society for Psychical Research*, 2 (1884), 191; 10 (1894), 2–8; 14 (1898), 3; Rose pp. 6–7. Radio techniques had engaged Kipling's attention since his cruise with the Channel Fleet in 1898, when the Navy had been experi-

menting with Marconi's new devices. 'If messages could pass through the impalpable "aether", as if material obstructions in space were of no account, why could not time be equally penetrable?' (quoted in Carrington, 1955, p. 375). See also 'Human Electricity', *Fortnightly Review*, May 1892, pp. 634–41. Many years later Kipling re-used the metaphor: 'I expect that every man has to work out his creed according to his own wave-length, and hope is that the Great Recovery Station is tuned to take *all* wave-lengths' (quoted in Carrington, 1955, p. 509).

5 For Kipling's description of his 'daemon' see Kipling (1937, pp. 208–10).

6 For definitions of theosophy see Hastings (1889); Blavatsky (1889); Sinnett (1881, 1883) and Olcott (1932, 1941). For Madame Blavatsky see Leonard (1976).

7 For the 'Egg' see Regardie (1932); Melchiori (1960) and Sewell (1935).

3

'*A light of blackness*':
The idiom of dream and paranoid fantasy

In the stories written in and after India, Kipling's continuing preoccupation with the antics of the inner self and with the fissures of personality is also revealed in his treatment of dream and paranoid fantasy. His early experiments with the uncanny – ghosts, magic and the supernatural – had arisen out of the experience of Empire. But the themes that follow through into the later works derive from a fascination with nervous and mental disorders in their own right. 'The Brushwood Boy', 'The Phantom Rickshaw', 'The House Surgeon', 'In the Same Boat' and 'The Dog Hervey' reflect the tradition of the 'psychological ghost story' or 'fictional psychiatry', which developed from Hoffmann, through Poe, Maupassant and James (see Briggs, 1977). These stories are fluid and dissembling. There is an analogy for their construction in Kipling's own account of how he came to write *Kim*:

> In a gloomy, windy autumn *Kim* came back to me with insistence, and I took it to be smoked over with my Father. Under our united tobaccos it grew like the Djinn released from the brass bottle, and the more we explored its possibilities the more opulence of detail we did discover. I do not know what proportion of an iceberg is below water-line, but *Kim* as it finally appeared was about one-tenth of what the first lavish specification called for. (1937, p. 139).

'The Brushwood Boy' (*TDW*) – Kipling's most elaborate dream story – shares a number of structural and thematic features with the supernatural stories: like them it draws upon similar aspects of recurrent imaginative fears. The story begins with a child, and although the narrative summarizes the customary training of a colonialist – George Cottar's progress through English public-school, Sandhurst and India – the imagination of childhood and the machinations of the 'City of Sleep' remain central to the story:

> She saw Georgie drown once in a dream-sea by the beach; . . . and he said as he sank: 'Poor Annie*an*louise! She'll be sorry for me now!' But 'Annie*an*louise,' walking slowly on the beach, called, ' "Ha! ha!" said the duck laughing,' which to a waking mind might not seem to bear on the situation.

The dream, or nightmare, in 'The Brushwood Boy' always begins on a road that runs along a beach near a pile of brushwood, but as the dream progresses the landscapes become alarming: 'dark purple downs . . . gardens all moist and dripping . . . mile-wide roaring rivers'. Georgie's rational waking response is to name and map out the territories and thereby control them. But as Zohreh Sullivan argues (1984, p. 226), the fear of submersion and the 'feminine' nature of the landscapes – the darkness and the water and the 'waiting Horror' of the 'Sick Thing' lying in bed in the innermost recesses of the dream – resemble the imaginative excess and the fear associated with Indian topography:

> They . . . crept into a huge house that stood, he knew, somewhere north of the railway station where the people ate among the roses. It was surrounded with gardens, all moist and dripping; and in one room, reached through leagues of whitewashed passages, a Sick Thing lay in bed. Now the least noise, Georgie knew, would unchain some waiting horror, and his companion knew it too; but when their eyes met across the bed, Georgie was disgusted to see that she was a child – a little girl in strapped shoes, with her black hair combed back from her forehead.

Finally, 'The Brushwood Boy' resembles the stories concerning ghosts, magic and the supernatural in its accommodation of violence – in this instance the sanctioned violence of dream: 'But the most amusing times were when he and she . . . walked through mile-long roaring rivers without even taking off their shoes, or set light to populous cities to see how they would burn.' But above all, what is significant and recurrent in these stories is the way the narratives work to disguise the unresolved traumas located within them. In the waking narrative of 'The Brushwood Boy' Georgie marries the princess of his dreams. But at the end of the story the notion of completion or closure is undermined by the hidden or dream narrative, which ends without a final meeting with or explanation of the Sick Thing. What lingers on in the reader's mind is not the supposed resolution in the coy and cloying engagement of the lovers, but echoes of a suppressed hysteria which counteracts the effect of narrative progression and fulfilment.

In this respect the stories of dream and paranoid fantasy enhance the experimental or 'Modernist' features of Kipling's writings already referred to. Kipling's use of the esoteric idiom of dream contributes to the stylistic intensity of his stories, their spatial form, their movement from discourse to image and their elegance and economy of meaning. The dream/fantasy structure combines immediacy and indirection in compelling ways, and the vivid compression of Kipling's treatment – fragmentation, distortion, displacement – is particularly suited to the representation of the self and its devious activities. Additionally, this kind of narrative places a special responsibility on the reader for, as in a dream, ordinary meanings are suspended and neither dreamer nor reader can claim a definitive interpretation. The process of reading, the relation between the reader and the text, involves an engagement with language and narrative structures which disguise rather than disclose their meaning. In each instance readers are invited to reinterpret the textual patterns according to their own apprehension of symbolic and emotional reality.

'The Phantom Rickshaw' (*WWW*), 'The House Surgeon' (*AR*), 'In the Same Boat' (*ADC*), 'The Dog Hervey' (*ADC*) and 'Friendly Brook' (*ADC*) reinforce the claims made in 'Wireless' and 'The Finest Story in the World' for imaginative literature to be a distinct kind of knowledge – a kind of knowledge whose veracity must be judged by its own terms. These stories celebrate a condition of verbal autonomy where the fiction has its own powers and forces independent of any mimetic or representational function. These stories also explore the relationship between creativity and mental illness, in which a disturbed or distorted angle of vision becomes an agent of creation and perception. At best, this kind of treatment reveals a potency in the everyday and the familiar – a rich revisioning, especially in respect of land-scape, of both rational and imaginative modes of perception. It is precisely the relationship between the images of dream, paranoid fantasy and imaginative vision that prompted Edmund Wilson's startling critical reassessment of Kipling's writings in 1928:

> It is the key to the whole of Kipling that the great celebrant of physical courage should convey his most moving and con-vincing effects in describing moral panic. The only authentic heroism in his work is the heroism of moral fortitude on the edge of collapse. (p. 93)

Kipling himself ended his catalogue of ghosts at the beginning of 'My Own True Ghost Story' with the cryptic remark: 'No native ghost has yet been authentically reported to have fright-ened an Englishman, but many English ghosts have scared the life out of both black and white.' In the early stories 'English ghosts' are frequently associated with blindness, which is also seen as symptomatic of breakdown. In 'Baa Baa, Black Sheep', the phan-tom shapes and shadows seen by Punch which 'cut him off from his world' are due to the failing sight which presages his collapse. In another sense, however, there is a relation between blindness and 'vision' in these stories: the images of paranoia are versions of authentic imaginative vision. The difference is that the language of breakdown and collapse is centred in the ego. Because it is the result of guilt, moral judgement and self-condemnation, the self remains locked in its anguish, in contrast to the fluidity of the creative and healing *open* imagination.

In 'The Phantom Rickshaw' Pansay's narrative records his belief that after his heartless desertion of Mrs Wessington, and his cruelty to her in her final illness, she and her coolies return to harry him into the grave: 'Here was I, Theobold Jack Pansay, a well-educated Bengal Civilian in the year of grace 1885, presum-ably sane, certainly healthy, driven in terror from my sweetheart's side by the apparition of a woman who had been dead and buried eight months ago.' By the end of the story Pansay is so transformed that the people around him have become 'impalpable fantastic shadows', and he admits that he is 'unhappy' whenever he is separated from his ghostly companion:

> Mrs Wessington spoke, and I walked with her from the Sanjaolie Road to the turning below the Commander-in-Chief's house as I might walk by the side of any living woman's rickshaw, deep in conversation . . . What we said during the course of that weird interview I cannot – indeed, I dare not – tell . . . It was a ghastly and yet in some indefinable way a marvellously dear experience. Could it be possible, I wondered, that I was in this life to woo a second time the woman I had killed by my own neglect and cruelty?

What is striking about this story is the completeness of Pansay's imaginative involvement with his guilt: it becomes the whole of his being and the whole of his life, and even, perhaps, brings about his death, as the final pages suggest. The doctor, Heatherlegh, bases his diagnosis on physical symptoms alone; but as the narrative progresses, Pansay's condition becomes so pathological that it would seem naive to speak of a cure, and impossible to imagine a return to 'reality'. Pansay's imagination has created another world out of guilt, to which that imagination and his whole being now belong. By his own admission, Pansay *is* guilty, but while the paranoid obsession *punishes* through a narrowing of vision, it also releases through an act of imaginative involvement. Pansay's 'conversation' and his courting of the ghostly Mrs Wessington are the 'marvellously dear experience' that he mentions, but that cannot be told. Thus in one sense the guilt reinforces the self, as when Pansay tries to hold himself together, to justify his actions, to forget the past, and to love Kitty. But in another sense his imagination works with that to create another mode of being, which is beyond the rational self (and dependent on its collapse) and which exists in another world in time. The frail, elusive figure of Mrs Wessington is the spirit child in 'They' seen through a glass darkly: the 'anima' or inspirational figure distorted into a nightmare. And there is no escape or no possibility of imaginative transformation because Pansay's imagination is centred in guilt and in unremitting self-punishment. In this respect, the world of the ghosts can be said to haunt the world of the living; they are felt to be separate, and to imprison the imagination in its own self-enclosed horror. In some sinister way this is reflected in the narrative itself, which becomes Pansay's way of telling himself into the event. It closes on the lines: 'For as surely as ever woman was killed by man, I killed Mrs Wessington. And the last portion of my punishment is even now upon me.' In this story fine discriminations between poet and 'anima', madman and hallucination, are erased.

'The House Surgeon', 'The Dog Hervey' and 'In the Same Boat' also reveal that aspect of Kipling's writing which deals – in Henry James's words – with 'the complicated soul' (1891, p. 163). In these stories Kipling remains preoccupied with the same kind of bizarre fantasies, distressed figures and disturbing encounters with the uncanny, but he now explores them in terms of neurosis and psychological trauma. Here an interest in psychological illness and in the unexpected potentialities of the mind takes precedence over purely ghostly themes. As D. M. E. Roskies indicates (1982, pp. 2–3), Kipling's 'forensic interest in states of mental anguish' and in their relief 'through a judicious ensemble of conversation and confrontation' resembles Freud's and is contemporaneous with the publication in England of *Studies in Hysteria* (1895) and *The Psychopathology of Everyday Life* (1901).[1] India is no longer a motivating element. The psychic force generated reveals the occult powers of the mind; it becomes a new way of experiencing the supernatural, and thus producing more convincing narrative modes.

In 'The House Surgeon', the innocent inhabitants of a house are haunted by an overwhelming sense of depression which descends unexpectedly and also at a certain hour, like 'a light of blackness . . . turned upon us' or 'the beam of a burning glass'. This is followed by the sensation of 'a live grief beyond words' and an unseen presence seeking to explain something vitally important. When this happens the occupants of the house say 'I beg your pardon' to each other, before they realize no one has spoken. The situation is resolved when the narrator persuades

Miss Moultrie, the previous owner of the house to revisit it. Miss Moultrie is a strict Evangelical who for many years believed that her younger sister's fall from a casement window was an act of suicide and bore the penalty of damnation. Miss Moultrie agrees to return to her old home when, after a narrow escape from a dangerous fall herself, she realizes that her sister's death could have been an accident. After her visit the spectre of anguish disappears and is replaced by a spirit of peace:

> It was a disgraceful evening. To say we rioted through the house is to put it mildly. We played a sort of Blind Man's Buff along the darkest passages, in the unlighted drawing-room, and the little dining-room, calling cheerily to each other after each exploration that here, and here, and here, the trouble had removed itself. We came up to *the* bedroom . . . and sat . . . drinking in blessed draughts of peace and comfort and cleanliness of soul.

At the end of the story we do not know what intimations Miss Moultrie has received, but it is clear that her obsessive brooding and its images of hatred was the product of Evangelical ideology. The narrator and the Moultries are also guilty of 'seeing' in these terms: '"It is nothing that we ourselves have ever done in our lives – that I will swear to you," said Mrs McLeod suddenly. "And we have changed our servants several times. So we know it is not *them*." . . . Meanwhile I rolled bread pills and counted my sins.' But throughout the story moral judgement is pitted against imaginative acceptance, just as Baxter's words recall the pagan god's acceptance of suicidal instincts in 'The Conversion of St Wilfrid' (*RF*):

> 'I don't know how it is with you, but my consolation is that God must know. He *must*! Things that seem on the face of 'em like murder, or say suicide, may appear different to God. Heh?'
>
> 'That's what the murderer and suicide can always hope –I suppose.'
>
> 'I have expressed myself clumsily as usual. The facts as God knows 'em – may be different – even after the most

clinching evidence. I've always said that – both as a lawyer
and a man, but some people won't – I don't want to judge
'em.'

This kind of 'seeing' is based in the imagination and is dependent
on intuition rather than concrete or factual proof. For this reason
it is entirely appropriate that the narrator and the McLeod's play
Blind Man's Buff in order to apprehend the new situation.
Perhaps this is why the narrator becomes increasingly aware that
the kind of evidence he is looking for is not tangible: 'I was more
bewildered than any Doctor Watson at the opening of a story', he
admits. Not longer after he finds himself among 'the ruins of my
black theories'. Indeed, the story's healing moves against the
narrative structure of the detective tale with its discoveries and
solutions: the moment of release is described in terms of the inner
activity of the mind – 'see the Shadow turned backwards' –
momentarily arresting the motion of the story and gathering it
to a single point.[2]
    The cure and the feeling of release at the end of the story are
perhaps structurally simple and too contrived, but the subtle and
disturbing examination of paranoid fantasy is one of Kipling's
most haunting evocations of the 'powers of darkness'. Here the
inner anguish is seen in terms of something that is known *before* it
is experienced and from which there is no escape. As the rational
mind is easily outstripped by immobilizing emotions inseparable
from anger and pain, any kind of self-defence becomes impossible:

And it was just then that I was aware of a little grey shadow,
as it might have been a snowflake against the light, floating
at an immense distance in the background of my brain. It
annoyed me, and I shook my head to get rid of it. Then my
brain telegraphed that it was the forerunner of a swift-
striding gloom which there was yet time to escape if I would
force my thoughts away from it, as a man leaping for life
forces his body forward and away from the fall of a wall. But
the gloom overtook me before I could take in the meaning of
the message. I moved toward the bed, every nerve already
aching with the foreknowledge of the pain that was to be

dealt it, and sat down, while my amazed and angry soul
dropped, gulf by gulf, into that Horror of great darkness
which is spoken of in the Bible, and which, as auctioneers
say, must be experienced to be appreciated.

'The arrows of our anguish / Fly farther than we guess' warns the
Rabbi in the poem that accompanies the story: the projection of
hatred and misery onto the innocent is no less painful for the fact
that the psychic influence is imposed unknowingly.

In 'The Dog Hervey' too, the narrator unwittingly finds himself employed as a detective, and arrives at a similar conclusion:
'It was all – all woman-work, and it scared me horribly.' In this
story, Moira Sichliffe projects the wraith of a sickly little dog into
the hallucinations of a drunkard, Shend, who had been kind to
her many years before. Through the 'psychic' influence she exerts
over both Shend and the narrator she causes Shend to return to
her. Her power is portrayed in the song she sings:

> I have no place apart –
> No dwelling more on sea or shore
> But only in thy heart.

Kipling describes her in an image like the one he had used to
describe Miss Moultrie: 'her face worked like glass behind driven
flame'; and leaves us in no doubt that she would stop at nothing:
'she would have fished my soul out of my breast on the instant',
the narrator says. Her environment, 'a mid-Victorian mansion of
peculiar villainy', is appropriate to her unconscious occult power.
It is not clear whether she, like the dog Hervey himself, is
'mentally afflicted' or 'a ghoul': several times the narrator is
moved to describe her as 'this woman beyond the decencies'. As
in 'The House Surgeon' parts of the story are opaque – particularly the role of Mrs Godfrey, who seems to act as an ally to Moira
Sichliffe but who is dead by the end of the story. As the narrator
himself admits, 'I don't know anything rational or reasonable
about any of it.' But what is interesting is the way the force of
Moira Sichliffe's anguish taps latent depths and abilities in the
psyche of those around her. At the beginning of the story this is
described in terms of forgetting:

some shadow of a word or phrase that kept itself out of
memory's reach as a cat sits just beyond a dog's jump.

with the air of one who had forgotten some matter of life and
death, which could be reached only by staring at me.

In this respect, the dog Hervey acts as a screen upon which
troubled and anarchic energies of the self are made visible:

> Now, in Malachi's eye I can see at any hour all that there is
> of the normal decent dog, flecked here and there with that
> strained half-soul which man's love and association have
> added to his nature. But with Hervey the eye was perplexed,
> as a tortured man's. Only by looking far into its deeps could
> one make out the spirit of the proper animal, beclouded and
> cowering under some unfair burden.

At times Hervey appears almost as the narrator's *doppelgänger*:
'Where I sat, he sat and stared, head stiffly slewed over one
shoulder in single-barrelled contemplation of me. He never gave
tongue, never closed in for a caress, seldom let me stir a step
alone.' Later in the story, when the narrator and Shend articulate
and share the hallucination of the dog, it loses its power: 'And
now – it's like a dream – a good dream, you know.' As in 'The
House Surgeon', the thing itself (Hervey) remains, but what has
changed are the connections with and reflections through him. By
a different arrangement of symbolic and emotional reality we see
'the long nightmare crumbling back into sanity' at the end of the
story when Hervey appears for the first time as a normal dog:

> Then the dog Hervey pranced out corkily from under the lee
> of a bench. Malachi, with one joyous swoop, fell on him as
> an enemy and an equal. Hervey, for his part, freed from all
> burden whatsoever except the obvious duty of a man-dog in
> his own ground, met Malachi without reserve or remorse,
> and with six months' additional growth to come and go on.

'In the Same Boat' extends further the suggestion implicit in
'The House Surgeon' and 'The Dog Hervey' that dream and fantasy are as essential a part of life as the conscious and rational
levels of the mind. In this story a peculiar authority – even a talis-

manic power – is given to the word 'imagine': 'You never *imagined* the thing. It was *laid* on you', says Nurse Blaber at the end. She is referring to the images of recurrent nightmare that have caused Conroy and Miss Henschil to become addicted to tranquillizers: 'These guarantee, on the label, "Refreshing and absolutely natural sleep to the soul-weary."' Conroy's image is of men dying in awful pain in the engine-room of a steamer; Miss Henschil's consists of leprous faces with mildew on them. For both the sequence of sounds and visual images culminate in a moment of awful shock: 'Suppose you were a violin-string vibrating – and some one put his finger on you? As if a finger were put on the naked soul!' Driven at last to consult 'nerve-specialists', the similarity of Conroy's and Miss Henschil's afflictions is revealed when the two consultants discuss the cases during a game of golf. Conroy's doctor is more speculative and imaginative in his therapy. His hypothesis is that the movement and new scenery offered by a train journey might dislodge the obsession, and he recommends that Conroy should take such a journey next time a visitation is imminent. He also suggests that Conroy should travel with Miss Henschil in the hope that they might be able to help and sustain each other. This begins the cure: through their companionship and their ability to verbalize the horror to each other, the nightmare is partly kept at bay. The healing is complete when the root cause of their neurosis is finally ascribed to pre-natal shock: the images of their nightmares derived from events that were witnessed by their mothers during pregnancy.

In its simplest terms the story describes the accommodation of the images of paranoia within the psyche: for when 'imagined' in a different context (actual happenings to their mothers) the images lose their capacity to terrify. But Kipling seems less interested in the medical diagnosis than in exploring the images themselves: these remain the same but their relocation in a new context of interpretation is a creative act which heals the mind. The narrative suggests that psychological complexes occur when images become 'locked' in the mind and 'soul': in this state imaginative response is static and frozen:

'But the cold feeling is beginning.'

'Lend it me, then.'

'And the drag down my right side. I shan't be able to move in a minute.'

'I can scarcely lift my arm myself,' said Conroy. 'We're in for it. . . . The two men moved like jointed dolls, and when their hands met it was as wood on wood.

The problem is that psychotic images have been mistaken for a kind of moral and psychological truth, some kind of judgement and punishment. The fact that the cure consists of freedom of thought and movement suggests the need for the images to be felt as protean rather than fixed. The suggestion is that interpretations are fantasies induced by the image, no more or less benign or threatening than the image itself.

In these stories the mystery of the conceptual, rational mind combines with the terrifying propensities of the imagination, and its susceptibility to insanity and its natural movement towards death: 'One's very soul – the soul one lives by – stopped.'

Conroy's and Miss Henschil's responses to the images of their dreams reflect a post-Enlightenment fear in the West of the grotesque and cruel images of fantasy (see Foucault, 1967). For Miss Henschil's mother, Skinner's 'Methody' sisters and Sir John Chartres, words and images have lost their vitality and power. Like 'the excellent tabloids' of M. Najdol their stale metaphors and comfortable clichés 'cover up the thing from being too real'. Paradoxically, the narrative shows how the words and images need to take on a subversive life of their own in order to restructure the ordinary and the normal. Kipling seems to be preoccupied with a similar theme in 'The Eye of Allah' (*DC*), where John of Burgos revitalizes Christian iconography – 'church-pattern devils' and 'green-stick virgins on the way to sainthood' – with figures that stand 'outside the rational mind': 'a raging, swaying background of woman-faced devils, each broke to and by her special sin, and each, one could see, frenziedly straining against the power that compelled her'. In both stories 'the worst' images are the most imaginatively vital – 'Life-created and rejoicing'. Their anarchic creative energy anticipates the mode of imagination advocated in 'The Bull that Thought' (*DC*).

In the final analysis, 'In the Same Boat', like 'The House Surgeon' and 'The Dog Hervey', operates as a collaborative fiction, putting all the disordered and traumatic events of 'life' into a new type of 'story'. In each story, the complexes remain as do the lacunae, but the reader's interpretation of these changes. The reader must not only discern patterns of signification and imagery, but must acknowledge their fundamental heterogeneity. He or she must reinterpret the patterns in the text, just as the characters in the stories reinterpret their own images and pre-occupations.

Elsewhere in Kipling's writings a dream-logic is strongly present in the treatment of landscape. In December 1902 he wrote to Rider Haggard: 'I am slowly discovering England which is the most wonderful foreign land I have ever been in' (Cohen, 1965, p. 51). *Puck of Pook's Hill, Rewards and Fairies*, 'An Habitation Enforced' (*AR*) and 'My Son's Wife' (*ADC*) suggest a mysterious, therapeutic re-ordering of the psyche, which displaces the neuroses induced by metropolitan culture.

The poems that preface or conclude these stories also evoke the powerful presence of the land. 'The Recall' describes the 'virtue' and 'magic' of the English earth, and 'A Charm', half-prayer and half-spell, characterizes the tone of all these writings:

> Lay that earth upon thy heart,
> And thy sickness shall depart!
>
> It shall sweeten and make whole
> Fevered breath and festered soul;
> It shall mightily restrain
> Over-busied head and brain
>
> .   .   .   .   .
>
> These shall cleanse and purify
> Webbed and inward-turning eye;
> These shall show thee treasure hid,
> Thy familiar fields amid.

In 'An Habitation Enforced', the American financier George Chapin has had a nervous breakdown. At the beginning of the story he and his wife Sophie move to a farm in a remote area of the southern English countryside. A part of the landscape they confront is characterized as alien to human constructions:

'No roads. No nothing!' said Sophie, her short skirt hooked by briars. 'I thought all England was a garden. There's your spire, George, across the valley. How curious!'

They walked towards it through an all-abandoned land. Here they found the ghost of a patch of lucerne that had refused to die; there a harsh fallow surrendered to yard-high thistles; and here a breadth of rampant kelk feigning to be lawful crop. In the ungrazed pastures swathes of dead stuff caught their feet, and the ground beneath glistened with sweat. At the bottom of the valley a little brook had under-mined its footbridge, and frothed in the wreckage. But there stood great woods on the slopes beyond – old, tall, and brilliant, like unfaded tapestries against the walls of a ruined house.

'All this within a hundred miles of London,' he said.

It is not that the entire countryside is waste. But the implication is that beneath the cultivated structure of even a lowland English landscape there abides a primeval power still able to reassert itself. Throughout the story the presentation of the rural myth of England and Englishness is sentimental and nostalgic, and works through an ahistorical universalizing poetic. The local community tacitly participates in this more than social, more than individual, power. The habits of leaving a room 'half-full of cotton bales' or of 'bending the course of the telegraph line' to avoid cutting down an elm-tree demonstrate the villagers' affinity with such a power. Similarly, Sophie Chapin is at first surprised at the way in which the villagers give priority to place over individual life:

'But why – why – did So-and-so do so-and-so?' Sophie would demand from her seat by the pothook; and Mrs Cloke would answer, smoothing her knees, 'For the sake of the place.'

'I give it up,' said George one night in their own room. 'People don't seem to matter in this country compared to the places they live in.'

The Americans initially express frustration at the ways and

attitudes of their new environment. George is obsessed by the lack of modern communications and both he and Sophie imagine they could manage the land more efficiently and make it more financially productive. The narrative is characteristically concerned with modes of apprehending and using knowledge. As George and Sophie stay longer in their new habitation the grip of metropolitan culture begins to lose its hold over them. George begins to respect another kind of knowledge or wisdom, a different view of time:

> 'How is one to know?' said George.
>
> 'Five years on from now, or so on, maybe, you'll be lookin' over your first year's accounts, and, knowin' what you'll know then, you'll say: "Well, Billy Beartup" – or Old Cloke as it might be – "did me proper when I was new." No man likes to have that sort of thing laid up against him.'
>
> 'I think I see,' said George. 'But five years is a long time to look ahead.'

Elsewhere in the story the kind of apprehension that does not insist upon immediate control of fact or meaning is seen to be therapeutic: 'The unhurried meals, the foreknowledge of deliciously empty hours to follow, the breadths of soft sky under which they walked together and reckoned time only by their hunger or thirst . . . – these things contented her soul and her body throve.' Such knowledge precedes the individual mind. It returns George and Sophie Chapin to something already present in their psyches, something which exceeds their psyches. Sophie is coming back to where she has already been, drawn to her ancestral home by psychic links that cannot be verified empirically:

> When she opened them she was looking at her mother's maiden name, fairly carved on a blue flagstone on the pew floor:
>
> Ellen Lashmar. ob. 1796. aetat. 27
>
> She nudged George and pointed. Sheltered, as they kneeled, they looked for more knowledge, but the rest of the slab was blank.

Notes

1   For reasons he outlined in *Something of Myself*, Kipling rarely passed
    comment on other writers. 'But Besant . . . advised me to "Keep out
    of the dog-fight." He said that if I were "in with one lot" I would
    have to be out with another; and that, at last, "things would get like
    a girls' school where they stick out their tongues at each other when
    they pass." For that reason, I have never directly or indirectly
    criticised any fellow craftsman's output, or encouraged any man or
    woman to do so' (1937, pp. 84–5). It would be interesting to know
    whether he had read Freud, and if so, what his views on Freud's
    writings were. Kipling's only reference to Freud in his writings
    occurs in his reference to Castorley's review of Manallace's book in
    'Dayspring Mishandled' (*LR*).
2   For similarities between the deductive practices of Sherlock Holmes
    and Freud see Shepherd (1985). See also n. 6 p. 81 below.

4

'Eyes readjustin' 'emselves':
Modernism and the pathology of war

'I cannot believe that James Joyce . . . would ever have written the Cyclops chapter of *Ulysses*, if he had never read Kipling', says Edmund Wilson in a review of Kipling's penultimate collection of stories, *Debits and Credits*.[1] This chapter considers Kipling's relationship to 'Modernism' (see Wilson, 1926, p. 194).

In the stories written after the war, and collected in *Debits and Credits* and *Limits and Renewals*, we see Kipling's continuing self-consciousness about writing and creative inspiration. The nine-year gap between the publication of *Debits and Credits* and its predecessor, *A Diversity of Creatures*, suggests that Kipling was pausing before setting out on the next phase of his literary career. During these years his readers began to express impatience with the growing complexity of his writings. In 1919 T. S. Eliot described him as 'a neglected celebrity . . . a laureate without laurels' (p. 297). He also suffered personal loss. There was inconsolable grief at the death of his son John in the Battle of Loos in 1915. His daughter Elsie's marriage in 1924 left Bateman's, the family home, 'resonant, silent and enormously empty'. He worried increasingly that his prolonged and undiagnosed illness might be cancer. In 1925 he wrote to Ernest Snow: 'You have my acutest sympathy over what you delicately call the "nuisance" of growing old. A train has to stop at some place or other. I only wish it wasn't such an ugly and lonesome place, don't you?' (Carrington, 1955, p. 503). The question of literary reputation recurs throughout the last two collections. In these volumes the concealed autobiographical elements, the references to his own art, and the musings on the past reputation, translation and current reception of classic texts – the Bible, Horace, Jane Austen – hint that Kipling was in the process of assessing his own literary career. In this respect the titles, *Debits and Credits* and *Limits and Renewals*, are strongly suggestive of an old man reviewing his own works. The stories and poems in both collections also reveal Kipling's continued preoccupation with certain key themes. They include tales of magic and the supernatural, historical material, farce and fantasies, and war. But one of the most striking aspects of the late stories is that they vindicate the techniques of Kipling's craft – almost as if depression and breakdown had been enabling. For example, as C. A. Bodelsen notes, in 'The Bull that Thought' (*DC*), the words 'art' and 'artist' occur fourteen times during the course of the story and the bullfighting scenes are described in terms that suggest a work of art and include a disquisition on its principles, its inspiration and the conditions necessary for its production.[2] By pointed comparisons between pre- and post-war conditions, the story also emphasizes the need for a widening of vision and for new fictional strategies to express the irrevocably altered conditions of life. 'After the War', the narrator says 'spaciously', 'everything is credible.' Both the frame and the narrative itself reaffirm Kipling's delight in the story well told and his conviction of its importance. As the narrator and Monsieur Voiron sit talking they drink a wine 'composed of the whispers of angels' wings, the breath of Eden and the foam and pulse of Youth renewed'.

'The Bull that Thought' is a story about a bull and a bullfight. Kipling counterbalances the linear sequence of the narrative by establishing an elaborate symmetry between the frame to the story and the story itself: the narrator beats the speed-record and Chisto is successful in the arena; both narrator and Chisto experience a return to youth and a renewed enthusiasm, and the analogy between the car and the bull suggests primitive energy contained or harnessed. What is also new here is the imaginative oddness of the story. In contrast to 'They', where, as one might expect, the anima or dispenser of inspiration is a child – shy, gentle and elusive – the bull's mixture of sensibility and callousness shocks and offends: 'My God, he was cruel! . . . He was playing for a laugh from the spectators which would synchronize with the fracture of the human morale', Monsieur Voiron says. The 'mathematically straight' rod of the story's frame is important here: the 'straight' power of the car is contrasted with the devious twistings of the bull and his cunning. Apis uses the side-kick, which is strictly dishonourable, and on several occasions contrives to murder as if by accident: 'In that instant, by that stumble, he produced the impression that his adorable assassination was a mere bestial blunder.' Divorced from morality, the bull becomes the instinctual artist who can play with all his passions and moods: he lives 'so many lives in one' because the daemon is not linked to a concept of single or unified personality. Apis's antics suggest that the creative act is not simply rational – that art issues from a confusion beyond intellectual control. His movements mime the deceit of all fictions: the artifice and circumlocution of narrative patterns. Like Yeats, who wrote in 'Nineteen Hundred and Nineteen' of 'the weasel's twist, the weasel's tooth', Kipling was fascinated by the cruel, even murderous, aspect of the creative imagination. But it is the cunning of artistic violence that fascinates Kipling, not its professional surge or frenzy, as in Yeats. As the bull performs his dance of death, Kipling inverts the process whereby images of creativity conceal under euphemism their powers of terror and destruction. 'Have you ever thought how I lie and steal daily on my travels – yes, and for aught you know, murder – to fetch you colours and earths?' asks John of Burgos in 'The Eye of Allah' (*DC*). These late stories support the teasing theoretical claim that the short story is in its nature cruel (see, for example, Bayley, 1987, p. 317). They also register a movement from a classic nineteenth-century model of growth through understanding to a Modernist emphasis on disjunction and solipsism. 'Mary Postgate' (*ADC*), for example, represents emotional development not as an expansion, but as a contraction of moral sympathy and wisdom. The difference, as Irving Howe points out, is an historical one: 'that a child can be killed from the air is a clear sign that the old familiar world is gravely threatened and new intolerable responses are needed. In extreme circumstances the inconceivable becomes conceivable' (1982, p. 34). We have already seen Kipling's fascination with the 'inconceivable' and the metaphorical significance of the child in his writing. In the late stories the threat to their, and his own, well-being, is inseparable from the fear of artistic failure and self-destruction. These negative energies would also throw light on Frank O'Connor's claim that the late stories 'go well beyond the normal capacity of the individual reader, either for laughter or tears'; that the reader finds himself asking ' "What is Kipling trying to do to me?" . . . and that if Kipling is a real writer, then there is something wrong with everybody else' (1965, p. 107).

In view of the techniques and qualities, range and complexity evident here, Edmund Wilson's remarks on the subject-matter in his 1926 review of *Debits and Credits* – 'how simple [Kipling's] ideas remain, how banal' – seem puzzling. But Wilson has fascinating things to say about what he regards as significant 'credits' in the technique and style, attributing to Kipling the invention of 'the whole genre of vernacular stories – I mean the kind in which we are made to see some comedy or tragedy through the half-obscuring veil of the special slang and technical vocabulary of the person who is telling it.' Wilson also comments on Kipling's 'unrivalled collection of . . . marvellous language exhibits: the kitchen chatter of a Sussex cook, the eloquence of a Middle Western realtor and several varieties of war slang' (1926, p. 194).

Wilson's commentary is important because the decreasing popularity of Kipling's writing in the 1920s was in part due to the increasing difficulty and obliquity of his writing. Kipling was above all alienated by his politics and by his reputation as a warmonger. The Liberal Press in particular waged a campaign against him, and the language games and metafictional practices of his fiction were just another nail in the coffin. Kipling's late stories share the literary self-consciousness of his Modernist contemporaries, but there are striking differences as well.

In *Something of Myself* Kipling tells us that he experimented with devices that would increase the complexity of his writing in *Rewards and Fairies*:

> I worked the material in three or four overlaid tints and textures, which might or might not reveal themselves according to the shifting light of sex, youth or experience. It was like working lacquer and mother-'o-pearl, a natural

combination, into the same scheme as niello and grisaille, and trying not to let the joins show. So I loaded up the book with allegories. (1937, p. 209)[3]

From this point onwards Kipling lengthened the time-span of his stories, moving from what Robert Louis Stevenson described as 'succint sketches and flying leaves of verse' (Green, 1971, p. 65) to stories which read like compressed novels (Tompkins, 1959, p. 4). He also experimented with structural effects: parallelisms between the frame and the story itself; narrators with different or conflicting perspectives; compression, symbolism and ambiguity. In these volumes covert structuring devices also include the framing of the collections between the first and last stories and the frequent necessity for expressing the same theme in a poem or story. Kipling's particular combination of poetry and prose lead T. S. Eliot to describe him as 'the inventor of a mixed form . . . a poem and a story together – or a story and two poems – combining to make a form which no-one has ever used in the same way, and in which no-one is likely to excel him' (1941, p. 42). The Definitive Edition of the poems is arranged according to themes as if designed to be read like a book of essays; and, as Richard Holmes has demonstrated, the autobiography is written in a modernist elliptical style and shaped around symbolic anecdote (1987, p. 10).

Kipling himself commented on the processes of composition by which he arrived at these textual effects: 'I have had tales by me for three or five years which shortened themselves almost yearly . . . a tale from which the pieces has been raked out is like a fire that has been poked', he remarks in *Something of Myself* (1937, p. 207). But importantly, as Lisa Lewis has demonstrated, Kipling decided at an early stage of composition not to allow his narratives any straightforward resolution (1986, pp. 53–5).

The indirection and ellipses of his writings troubled many of his readers – a bewilderment and indignation epitomized in the words of Lord Radcliffe's address to the Kipling Society in 1986:

[Kipling's] late manner . . . often fails to make effect . . . by the sheer complexity of the structure, the dedication to jargon, the withdrawal . . . After all, prose must remain an art of communication . . . The artist has no right to retire so far that only through prayer and fasting can his voice be heard. (Birkenhead, 1980, p. 337)[4]

But Kipling is not really a ludic artist, for all his interest in games and ritual. The most interesting and unusual aspect of the Modernist self-consciousness in his stories is its co-existence with the pressure of personal feeling. As Frank O'Connor remarked of 'Baa Baa, Black Sheep': 'Chekhov, the Doctor, can face the fact that little chaps go blind, and mad, and desperate. Kipling can't' (1965, p. 111). The *descente aux enfers* had been imaginatively anticipated in the early stories of psychic and psychological trauma, but the suffering related to the experiences of war is at once more extensive and more devastating. 'Oh, there was fun in Hell, those days, wasn't there, boys?' quips Bevin in 'A Friend of the Family'. But, after the event, the shattered war veterans find themselves dealing with imaginative processes that have restructured their daily lives into new shapes – surreal or emotional tableaux. 'Ye-es,' says Pole (in the same story), 'The trouble is there hasn't been any judgement taken or executed. That's why the world is where it is now. We didn't need anything but justice – afterwards. Not gettin' that, the bottom fell out of things, naturally.'

In a number of the stories written between 1918 and 1920 Kipling explores the new mental horrors provided by the war: 'unburiable things' which 'immobilise' the victims 'from the soul outwards'. The symptoms of shell-shock were surprisingly similar to the nervous disorders of peacetime. And war neuroses cause Kipling once again to explore the problems caused by a contradiction between two lives – returning to the experiences of alienation, relativity and the illusory status of the ideological concept of self and nation that form so strong a narrative thread in the early Indian, and in the pre-war stories. In the post-war stories the limits of individual identity are, again, uncertain. As the official, socially ratified roles break down there is only a narrow divide between healing images and the images of paranoia. 'Why anything – Jack the Ripperism or religious mania – might come uppermost', Keede (the fictional doctor) remarks in 'Fairy Kist'

(*LR*). In this story and in 'The Woman in His Life' (*LR*) and 'The Miracle of St Jubanus' (*LR*), the nocturnal landscapes of war and the sense of movement – or stasis – in a threatened space provide Kipling with a new perspective on the self expressed in dreams and in neurotic symptoms, and on the images of an un-accommodated self that assume terrifying shapes. As Eric Leed points out in his study of combat and identity in the First World War:

> In war men were estranged from their societies, and one must take this estrangement literally: they were 'made' strange to the men and things of their past, and made strange to themselves. In the words of Gorch Jachs, who died in the offensives of 1918 . . . 'I have become a riddle to myself, and often shudder at myself, am terrified at myself.' (1979, p. 4)

Writing about war led Kipling again to experiment with space and time. The landscapes of the war stories, like those of the dream stories discussed in Chapter 3, are peculiarly sexual. The war narratives also return Kipling to his habitual preoccupations with the conflict between private desire and public duty, and the tense equilibrium between victims and victimizers.

Historians have suggested that the suppression of consciousness necessary for survival in the trenches inspired strong fantasies of modes of release, and a corresponding need for security and reassurance. The consciousness native to the modern industrial-ized war is paradoxically, as Eric Leed notes, magical and ritual-istic, working on the basis of

> analogies and associations that presume a multivalent world of significances . . . This state was often described in terms of a loss of coherence and the disappearance of any sense of temporal sequence. It created the setting for irrational thoughts and unbidden associations . . . The circumstances of war produced a notion that the relation between individ-uals and the forces that governed them was much closer to magic. (1979, pp. 129, 127; see also Fussell)

In that the Front assimilated life to death and destroyed any sense

of individual agency, trench warfare took on an aspect of the
uncanny – an experience of horrible enchantment whose rules
were learned through paradox and shock. War but devalued
existing ideologies. The collapse of categories and continuities
encouraged the resurgence of liminal, archaic mentalities. Many
veterans would later describe their experiences in elevated, even
mystical and religious terms.

A number of Kipling's late stories, including 'In the Interests
of the Brethren', 'The Janeites' (*DC*) and 'A Madonna of the
Trenches' (*DC*) show Kipling first turning to the 'magic' and
'ritual' of Freemasonry to find the restorative balance he seeks.[5]
There had been scattered references to Freemasonry in the early
works, but these stories are actually placed in the fictional lodge
'Faith and Works 5837'. 'I sat between a one-footed RAMC
Corporal and a Captain of the Territorials, who, he told me, had
"had a brawl" with a bomb, which had sent him in two directions'
the narrator tells us in 'In the Interests of the Brethren'. This is
the first story in which we meet injured and shell-shocked men.
Located in London during the First World War, it portrays a
Masonic Lodge of Instruction which has offered its hospitality to
the injured Masons in local hospitals. The presiding officers are
selected from among the wounded and crippled and perform the
ceremony as well as they can: 'it's the Spirit, not the Letter, that
giveth life' Burges says. During the course of the evening the
men's minds are healed by companionship:

> The one-footed RAMC on my right chuckled.
> 'D'you like it?' said the Doctor to him.
> '*Do* I? It's Heaven to me, sittin' in Lodge again. It's all
> comin' back to me now, watching their mistakes . . . Yes,
> "veiled in all'gory and illustrated in symbols" – the Father-
> hood of God, an' the Brotherhood of Man; an' what more in
> Hell *do* you want?'

Kipling had previously written admiringly in 'In the Presence'
(*ADC*) of the precise ritual observance on the part of the Sikh
brothers and the Gurkha orderlies. The rehearsal of ceremony in
'In the Interests of the Brethren' leads the narrator to say that he
'realised for the first time what word-and-gesture-perfect ritual

can be brought to mean'. His perception is reinforced by Burges,
who remarks: 'All Ritual is fortifying. Ritual's a natural necessity
for mankind. The more things are upset, the more they fly to it.'

'In the Interests of the Brethren' is not really a story; it is more
like a narrative sketch of exhausted veterans seeking a reprieve
from the pressures of war: a context which enables Kipling to explore Freemasonry as a possible technique of healing. But three
later stories written between 1927 and 1930 and published in
Limits and Renewals, focus on war neuroses that have taken years
to surface. 'Fairy Kist', 'The Woman in his Life' and 'The
Miracle of St Jubanus' reveal an intensification of pathological
fantasy which refuses to be repressed, transformed, cured or
understood. In these stories Kipling experiments with narrative
structures compatible with the incongruity between meaning and
actuality that characterized war. He also explored further the
kinds of imaginative processes that restructure the 'ordinary'
thought processes of daily life. As in 'The House Surgeon', the
cure is effected through some kind of repetitive re-enactment of
the experience behind the symptom.

At the centre of 'Fairy-Kist' is Wollin, who has survived
'shrapnel-peppering . . . gassing . . . gangrene', but is now, long
after the war, tormented by 'horrible dope dreams' and 'Voices'
which demand that he 'must go and plant roots and things at
large up and down the countryside'. Although he is a keen
gardener, the Voices, 'a whole Army Corps shouting in his ears',
terrify him. The only way to maintain any kind of stability is to
follow their instructions as that seems to silence them. One day
when Wollin is out planting he stumbles over the dead body of
Ellen Terry. Keede, driving past in his car at that moment,
assumes Wollin to be the murderer, and is able to track him down
because he remembers the number of his motorbike and identifies
a trowel in Wollin's house identical to that left beside Ellen's
body. Meanwhile, supposing nobody will believe in his 'Voices',
Wollin prepares to commit suicide, the alternative being imprisonment in Broadmoor. As it happens, however, it turns out
that Ellen was accidentally killed by the whiplash from a passing
lorry and Wollin is freed from suspicion. He is also liberated from
the 'Voices' when they are re-interpreted by Keede and Lem-

ming. Using the evidence at their disposal, they demonstrate how the haunting images and commands represent a nightmare version of Mrs Ewing's 'Mary's Meadow':

> a long nursery-yarn about some children who planted flowers out in a garden that wasn't theirs, so that such as had no gardens might enjoy them, and one of the children called himself an Honest Root-gatherer, and one of 'em had something like water on the brain; and there was an old squire who owned a smiling bull-terrier that was fond of the children, and he kept his walnuts till they were rotten, and then he smashed 'em all. (Ewing, 1886)

It is a harmless and rather beautiful story, but when it was read to Wollin during an air-raid in the war it got mixed up with 'pain and . . . dope . . . bombings and nightmares', lodged in a corner of his mind, and took charge. The way in which 'the best, the kindest, the sweetest, the most eenocent tale' works on unknown parts of the imagination is endorsed by passing reference throughout the story to states of mind and powers beyond the province of science. The reference to the ECF – 'the Eclectic *but* Comprehensive Fraternity for the Perpetuation of Gratitude towards Lesser Lights' – at the beginning is clearly ironic. But the Housekeeper, the woman at Barnet Horse Fair and Lilly the Astrologer are all in touch with the occult. As with Conroy and Miss Henschil in 'In the Same Boat', identification of the causes of Wollin's 'Voices' makes them disappear. However, his suffering is proportionately worse than that of the characters in the earlier story: 'He was burned out – all his wrinkles gashes, and his eyes readjustin' 'emselves after looking into Hell . . . a ghost that gnawed itself.' The added danger in which he stands is reflected in the incurable insanity of Jimmy Tigner, who is destroyed by the same random sequence of events by which Wollin is saved. Like the speaker in 'The Mother's Son', the poem that prefaces the story, he is unable to free himself from the images of his obsession:

> I have a dream – a dreadful dream –
> A dream that is never done

It is possible that in 'Fairy Kist' Kipling was not only continuing the process of re-invigorating images begun in 'In the Same Boat' and 'The Eye of Allah', but also trying to re-invent narrative forms: Wollin is compelled to tell his story against his own inclination 'just like the Ancient Mariner'. And if 'Fairy Kist' is dependent on images from a children's story seen from different perspectives, it also seeks to explore and revise the framework of the detective tale. 'I wish I could do a decent detective story', says the narrator at the beginning; police and reporters feature in the background 'looking for clues', and Keede's prognoses centre on 'Jack the Ripper': 'my theory was that my car had frightened the brute off before he could do anything in that line'. But in the tale that is told, the 'detectives', a doctor and his Masonic friend, are obliged to admit that 'we were not a success as man-hunters' nor 'exactly first class Sherlocks'. Their role is rather to act as 'magicians', whose reframing of the narrative will shape the victimizing voices back into the innocent figures of 'Mary's Meadow':

> 'He used the words "root-gathering". It's an unusual combination nowadays,' said Lemming suddenly. 'That made me take notice'

> 'he used the word "Paradise". Then Will asked him if he could give the precise wording of his orders to plant things. He couldn't do that either. Then Will said, like a barrister: "I put it to you, that the Voices ordered you to plant things by the wayside *for such as have no gardens* . . . Now for your dog. I put it to you that the smiling dog was really a secret friend of yours'

> '*Mary's Meadow*!' Sandy's hand banged the table. 'Hsh!' said Burges, enthralled. 'Go on, Robin.'

The plot is resolved by a recasting of the narrative within a benign frame of reference. Doctor and detective join forces to interpret the unsuspected significance of minor details.[6] The narrative enterprise involved here supports W. H. Auden's speculation that:

> The fantasy . . . which the detective story addict indulges is the fantasy of being restored to the Garden of Eden, to a

state of innocence, where he may know love as love and not as the law. The driving force behind this daydream is the feeling of guilt, the cause of which is unknown to the dreamer. The fantasy of escape is the same, whether one explains the guilt in Christian, Freudian, or any other terms. One's way of trying to face the reality, on the other hand, will, of course, depend very much on one's creed. (1963, p. 158)

'Fairy Kist' has been criticized for its overschematic plot, and a reductive simplification of the human response to pain and guilt (see Mallett, 1987, pp. 11–14). But the story does not work with an empirical measure of the true and the false. It deals with apprehensions where the opposite of truth is not error, but another kind of imaginative truth. In this respect it seems entirely appropriate that 'Fairy Kist' ends not with the arrest and conviction of a murderer but with three men sitting together at a table while one of them says 'Now I'll tell you a story . . .'.

In 'The Woman in his Life' extreme inner tension finds its expression in bizarre and frightening images: first 'a full-size red and white bullock, dancing in a tea-cup'; then 'a small dog, pressed against the skirting board of his room – an inky fat horror with a pink tongue . . . it began as a spreading blur, which morning after morning became more definite'. These appear to John Marden after a bout of overwork which triggers latent fears and obsessions. Both bullock and dog dramatise the sense of being watched from within by the shadows of the mind in personified guises. Marden himself recognizes that the 'bullock' can be traced back to an advertisement which 'had caught the tail-end of his eye', and, in the shape of a hallucination, suddenly 'stood up before him'. There is no immediate source for the dog, but as the story proceeds we realize that it is an image onto which Marden projects 'every forgotten and hardly held back horror' of the trenches: two years' experience as a sapper beneath the Messines ridge during the war:

It was better than the ox in the tea-cup, till it was borne in on John Marden one dawn that, if It crawled out into the centre of the room, the Universe would crash down on him.

In order to try and break Marden's obsession with the phantom dog, his batman Shingle buys him a real dog, Dinah. As Marden struggles to distinguish between the two his comments reveal his own divided self, split between conscious and unconscious reaction, terror and control:

> 'It's coming out into the room,' roared the first. 'Now you've *got* to be mad! Your pistol – before you make an exhibition of yourself!'
> 'Call it, you fool! Call it!' the other commanded
>
> 'Right! All right! A cold nose is the sign of a well dog. It's all right! It's alive!'
> 'No. It's *come* alive!' shouted the first. 'It'll grow like the bullock in the cup! Pistol!'
>
> 'No – no – alive! Quite alive!' the other interrupted . . .
> 'Shovel! – *Not* pistol! Get the shovel, you ass!'

As Marden gets used to having Dinah around, the responsibility for looking after her steadies him and lessens his fear of 'that Other'. The process of healing continues as he projects his stifled 'normal' feelings and emotions onto Dinah. What is fascinating is the way she *becomes* his moods, just as the pathological sides of his personality are focused onto her shadow:

> She was by turns, and in places, arrogant, imbecile, coy, forthcoming, jealous, exacting, abject, humorous, or apparently stone-cold . . . When she trotted back, That Other took shape again behind her, but John felt relieved.

Marden's cure is completed when Dinah gets trapped in an old badger's earth. In order to save her, Marden crawls underground again and is forced to face the suppressed terror of 'his two years underground work . . . with the imagined weight of all earth overhead!' As he pushes himself through the narrow tunnel, 'widening the bottle-necked passage with his spade', he re-experiences the war, voluntarily and cathartically: 'He pushed himself over a last pit of terror, and touched her.' As Marden projects himself into the past he frees himself from its horror: 'I've got it off the books now. It's behind me!'

In this story it seems significant that Marden literally journeys underground. Like the two dogs, upper and lower worlds are metaphors for the mind/imagination seen from different perspectives. These are coexistent and synchronic, but one is seen from above and in the light, the other from below and in the darkness. The 'underground' or 'shadow' self stalks the conscious mind and is inseparable from it, and tunnel and dog remind us of the flickering patterns within reality.

For Martin Ballart, too, in 'The Miracle of St Jubanus', the 'nail of his obsession' is an image: 'One of those cursed Kodak pictures, of a young man in a trench, dancing languorously with a skeleton'. For him as well, return to his home and place of work do not 'restore'. Moments of respite are brief intermissions before being 'visibly replunged in his torments'. The old village padre despairs of his recovery and describes him to the narrator as a boy 'descending alive into Hell'. He goes on to explain the 'darkness of soul' in terms of being 'split open': for Ballart, as for Wollin and Marden, distinctions between outer and inner, conscious and unconscious, are suspended. Like 'The Mother's Son', Ballart remains fixed in horror – 'blasted, withered, dumb – a ghost that gnawed itself' – because he cannot tell of it. 'You call them *Mick-robs*. We call them Devils', the Padre says to the narrator. 'The living damnation' of Ballart and others like him represents an intensification of Kipling's earlier explorations of 'the powers of darkness'.

In this story, the cure is effected through the freeing of the image. When two acolytes dressed for Mass and the atheistical schoolmaster get hooked up in the split whalebone of the padre's umbrella, 'the central effect, Monsieur, was that of an undevout pagoda conducting a *pas de trois* in a sacred edifice'. At this moment the image of 'the young man . . . dancing languorously with a skeleton' merges in Ballart's mind with the comic movements of the skeletal frame of the umbrella and its unwilling captives, as it 'promenaded through pagan undulations and genuflexions'. As life and imagination join in a moment of synchronicity, Martin's involuntary laughter breaks his obsession, and in a now familiar pattern his imaginal self is revealed through integration and movement:

'It is said that I was on my knees beating my forehead against the back of a *prie-dieu*, when we heard, above all, the laugh of Faunus himself – the dear, natural voice of my Martin, rich with innocent delight, crying: "But, do it again! If you love me, Uncle Falloux, do it all again!"'

Notes

1   For Joyce on Kipling see Ellman (1959, pp. 244, 263).
2   For detailed analyses of 'The Bull that Thought' see Bodelsen (1964, pp. 53–72) and Gilbert (1972, pp. 168–87).
3   See Holmes (1987, pp. 10–11). Kipling's descriptions of his writing in terms of painting and engraving are well known. Holmes suggests that further hints on Kipling's attitude to writing may be found in the little-known essay 'Some Aspects of Travel' (1914) (*ABW*) where Kipling compares writing to the experience of explorers, and to the logistical pressures of organizing an expedition into unknown territory.
4   See James's letter to Grace Norton, 25 December 1897: '[Kipling's] ballad future may still be big. But my view of his prose future had much shrunken . . . In his earliest time I thought he perhaps contained the seeds of an English Balzac; but I have given that up in proportion as he has come down steadily from the simple in subject to the more simple – from the Anglo-Indians to the natives, from the natives to the Tommies, from the Tommies to the quadrupeds, from the quadrupeds to the fish, and from the fish to the engines and screws' (Green, 1971, p. 69).
5   For discussions on Kipling and Freemasonry see Frost (1942); Bazely (1949); Smith (1926) and Carr (1964).
6   For the relationship between psychoanalysis and the detective story see Shepherd (1985). See also G. K. Chesterton's priest-detective Father Brown, *Father Brown: Selected Stories* (OUP, 1971).

5

'Your cold Christ and tangled Trinities':
The critique of Christian discourse

From the beginning of Kipling's career the nature of his religious belief and its effect on his writings were the subject of critical controversy. In an article entitled 'The Religion of Mr Kipling', published in 1898, W. B. Parker wrote: 'The appearance of Mr Kipling's Recessional Hymn may well be considered one of the chief religious events of the past two years' (p. 662). The poem in question voices a concern over the potential abuse of power in the Empire by means of a Christianity too closely interwoven with commerce and imperialism. 'Lest we forget – Lest we forget', runs the refrain of 'Recessional'. 'Dominion over palm and pine' is represented as incompatible with 'An humble and a contrite heart'. But 'Recessional' could also be regarded as a celebration of Empire – its sombre majesty exceeding the critique of an arrogant and patriotic Christianity. 'Hardly any other piece of verse written in our day has been so quickly and widely taken up', wrote J. T. Sunderland in 1899 (p. 608). The majority seemed to favour a reading of the poem as jingoistic. And if some, like W. B. Parker, or Harry Ward in the *Methodist Review* of 1900, discerned a vein of religious conviction beneath Kipling's masculine Freemasonry of adventure, others criticized Kipling's stories as 'devoid of spiritual uplift' and 'divorced from all moral judgements and values' (*Independent*, 1899, 51, pp. 888–91; Gardiner, 1899). In 1891 and 1893 reviewers of *Life's Handicap* and *Many Inventions* warned 'ladies' reading circles' off these volumes and expressed the view that 'the demands of Christian feeling may be violated by the writings'.[1] In 1900, a reviewer for the *Outlook* asked: 'Is there a single instance of high and holy love of anything in [Kipling's] works?' (p. 216). Charges of 'muscular Paganism' and 'the philosophy of a barbarian' were to follow (*Bookman*, 1901; *Harper's Bazaar*, 1901, p. 796). In the most aggressive contemporary attack, 'The Voice of the Hooligan', Buchanan described Kipling's manner as 'raving in capital letters about the Seraphim and the pit . . . a Cockney "gawd" requisitioned for the purposes of blasphemy and furious emphasis' (Gilbert, 1965, pp. 23, 26).

But Kipling's use of the Bible and Christian doctrine in his writings refutes the claim that he was ignorant of either. Although his parents were not practising Christians, there was a strong tradition of Methodism in his family. His grandfathers, the Rev. Joseph Kipling and the Rev. George Browne Macdonald, were both Methodist ministers.[2] His own earliest acquaintance with the Bible came by way of punishment exercises at Lorne Lodge: 'I learned most of the Collects that way and a great deal of the Bible', he tells us in his autobiography (1937, p. 11). The knowledge stayed with him at school, and beyond. In India in March 1888 Edmonia Hill noted in her diary: 'No one is more apt than [Kipling] with appropriate Biblical quotations, as all can see' (p. 408). Some years later he wrote to Edward Lucas White asking him to consider for publication stories centred around the Bible: 'a set of things . . . [including] David eating the Shewbread (which is a splendid episode), Jonah cursing beneath the withered gourd and a few other matters' (Ross, 1987, p. 22). From 1899 to 1925 the regular correspondence between Kipling and Rider Haggard suggests that Kipling continued to read the Bible and biblical commentaries for the rest of his life. The following letter, dated 21 February 1925, is a characteristic example:

Now I *know* (I've just been doing my Sunday reading) that of all the lies Paul told, his statement (or implication) that he suffered 'em gladly was the biggest. He didn't – by a damn sight. It soured the little man badly . . . Which reminds me, what do you make of the intended significance of Jahveh saying that He'd 'put His Hand' over Moses when He hid him in a cleft of the rock, against the blaze of his glory?

I can't see what was in the translator's mind. (Cohen, 1965, pp. 136–7)

Kipling, usually so reticent about the processes of composition, himself acknowledged the influence of the idiom and rhythms of the King James Bible on his prose style. 'If you go no further back than the Book of Job you will find that letters, like the art of printing, were born perfect', he tells us (1928, p. 37); and in *Proofs of Holy Writ* he gives imaginative expression to his belief that the King James Bible represents the perfection of English speech.[3] In this story the Rev. Miles Smith of Brasenose College, Oxford, sends passages from Ezekiel and Jeremiah to Shakespeare and asks him to perfect their English. As Shakespeare engages Ben Jonson in the debate, it is as if Kipling is trying to recreate the processes by which first Tyndale and Coverdale, and their early Jacobean scholars produced what Kipling believed to be the finest translation of the Bible. In the following extract Shakespeare explains his task to Ben Jonson:

> The King has set all the scholars of England to make one Bible, which the Church shall be bound to, out of all the Bibles men use . . . Miles Smith . . . and halfscore others, his cloth, are cast to furbish up the Prophets – Isaiah to Malachi. In his opinion by what he's heard, I had some skill in words, and he'd condescend . . . to inquire o' me privily, when direct illumination lacked, for a tricking out of his words or the turn of some figure . . . But, Ben, ye should have heard my Ezekiel making mock of fallen Tyrus in his twenty-seventh chapter. Miles sent me the whole, for, he said, some small touches. I took it to the Bank – four o'clock of a summer morn; stretched out in one of the wherries – and watched London Port and Town, up and down the river, waking all arrayed to heap more upon evident excess. Ay! 'A merchant for the people of many isles' . . . 'The ships of Tarshish did sing of thee in thy markets'? Yes! I saw all Tyre before me neighing her pride against lifted heaven (pp. 334–54)

Other stories reveal an equally strong interest in the Bible, as Ann Weygandt has shown:

Genesis is constantly used; there are innumerable allusions
to the Garden of Eden, the fall, Cain, Noah and Joseph . . .
the stories of Samson and David apparently had a strong
appeal, and allusions to Naaman, Gehazi, and the house of
Rimmon occur again and again. There is scarcely an incident in the Gospels that fails to be noted and Kipling's keen
interest in the character of St Paul is proved in . . . many independent references to Acts and the Epistles. Job, the
Psalms and Isaiah were his favorites among the poetical
books, and all the books of wisdom – Proverbs, Ecclesiastes,
and the Apocryphal Ecclesiasticus – are frequently cited.[4]

The most interesting play of discourses in relation to that of
Christianity occurs in poems like 'A Nativity', 'Gethsemane',
and 'The Sons of Martha', written during the First World War.
This familiarity with – even immersion in – the fables and
rhetoric of the Bible also feeds into Kipling's continually shifting
and modifying religious or spiritual perspectives in the stories.

From *Plain Tales from the Hills* to *Rewards and Fairies*, his stories
question nineteenth-century Evangelical Christianity, and challenge the proselytizing, educational and philanthropic motives of
Church Missions:[5] 'The Conversion of St Wilfrid' (*RF*) is rep-
resentative of this challenge, and recalls the missionary tales in
the earlier collections (*Plain Tales from the Hills* to *Many Inventions*).
As in 'Lispeth', 'The Judgement of Dungara' and 'The Limitations of Pambe Serang', the indigenous population pretend to
be converted for material gain: St Wilfrid voices his 'shrewd
suspicion' that the 'real motive' for conversion was to get a good
harvest. 'The sick and the maimed will profess any and every
creed for the sake of healing and will laugh at you because you are
simple enough to believe them', the narrator of 'The Judgement
of Dungara' had said. 'The Conversion of St Wilfrid' also offers
an example of the kind of clergymen previously encountered in
'Lispeth', 'The Record of Badalia Herodfoot' (*MI*) and in *Kim*.
The Chaplain Eddi is overbearing and narrow-minded and
Meon's teasing reveals the limitations of his belief:

'That's not fair,' said Meon. 'You call [the seal] a demon
and a familiar spirit because he loves his master and likes

music, and when I offer you a chance to prove it, you won't take it. Look here! I'll make a bargain. I'll be baptised if you'll baptise Padda too. He's more of a man than most of my slaves.' . . . My good Eddi must have been a little over-tired with his day's work. 'I am a servant of the Church,' he cried. 'My business is to save souls, not to enter into fellow-ship, and understandings with accursed beasts.'

But rather than merely exposing the hypocritical and uncharitable behaviour of the Christians, the story records the 'conversion' of both Eddi and St Wilfrid to a spiritually richer, more tolerant belief. 'The Conversion of St Wilfrid' opens out to an affirmation of the need for a broader spiritual sense, a redefined Christianity, which can accommodate the non-Christian (Meon). What the Christians come to understand, through their friendship with the pagan scholar Meon, and after a narrow escape from death at sea, is the need for absolute compassion: 'I had learned a great deal', St Wilfrid tells Dan and Una at the end. 'One should deal kindly with all the creatures of god and gently with their masters. But one learns late.' As Eddi's belief develops, he begins to love the seal, asking its forgiveness for 'earlier grievances' and calling it 'my little brother'. In 'The Conversion of St Wilfrid' Eddi's new-found humility and courtesy provide a marked contrast to the attitude of the Yorkshire Chapel-folk in 'On Greenhow Hill' who had continued to exclude Learoyd's dog from their belief: 'They said I mun give him up 'cause he were worldly and low; and would I let mysen be shut out of heaven for the sake of a dog.' Learoyd's uncertainty and sensitivity to his own exclusion are also touchingly rendered:

But I niver had nowt to say for mysen, though there was a deal o' shoutin', and old Sammy Strother, as were almost clemmed to death and doubled up with the rheumatics would sing out, 'Joyful! Joyful!' and 'at it were better to go up to heaven in a coal-basket than down to hell i' a coach an' six. And he would put his poor old claw on my shoulder, sayin' 'Doesn't tha feel it tha great lump? Doesn't tha feel it?' An' sometimes I thought I did, and then again I thought I didn't, an' how was that? . . . And i' th' class meetings they said as I mun have some experiences to tell, and I hadn't a word to say for mysen.

Here, as in a number of the stories, Kipling would seem to express a preference for the precepts and practices of Roman Catholicism. 'I hold by the Ould Church,' Mulvaney says:

> for she's the mother av them all – ay, an' the father too. I like her bekaze she's most remarkable rig'mintal in her fittings. I may die in Honolulu, Nova Zambia or Cape Cayenne, but wherever I die, me bein' fwat I am, an a priest handy, I go under the same ordhers an' the same wurruds an' the same unction as tho' the Pope himsilf come down from the roof av St Peter's to see me off. There's neither high nor low, nor broad nor deep, nor betwixt nor between wid her, an' that's fwat I like.

But Kipling was critical of what he regarded as Catholicism's tendency to prey on the fear of Divine punishment. In 'The Mutiny of the Mavericks' (*LH*), Mulvaney describes his mother 'starting from her sleep with shrieks to pray for a husband's soul in torment'. And even in 'On Greenhow Hill' Mulvaney's praise is highly qualified:

> But mark you, she's no manner av Church for a wake man, bekaze she takes the body and sowl av him, onless he has his proper work to do. I remimber when my father died that was three months comin' to grave; begad, he'd ha' sold the shebeen above our heads for ten minut's quittance av purgathory. An' he did all he cud. That's why I say ut takes a strong man to dale with the Ould Church.

In 'The Conversion of St Wilfrid', on the other hand, Kipling points to areas of religious experience that transcend the language of dogma or creed and may be experienced by all believers. References at the beginning of 'The Conversion of St Wilfrid' to the 'soft lacey tunes' of the organ, and the altar-gates which never close, and to 'the broad gentle flood of the main tune' at the end of the story contrast with the random killing that frames 'On Greenhow Hill'. 'The Conversion of St Wilfrid' suggests that

nobody has the right to criticize another's faith, and that the
impulse to conversion must be heartfelt and willing. 'No God in
any Heaven shall say that I came to him or left him because I was
wet and cold', Meon says to St Wilfrid, and he claims to be converted only *after* St Wilfrid counsels him to stand by his own gods.

> You can tell your mates that even in that place, at that time,
> hanging on the wet, weedy edge of death, our Bishop, a
> Christian, counselled me, a heathen, to stand by my fathers'
> gods. I tell you now that a faith which takes care that every
> man shall keep faith, even though he may save his soul by
> breaking faith, is the faith for a man to believe in.

In 'Letters of Marque' Kipling's description of a young priest
who 'giggled deprecatingly at his own creed every time he was
questioned about it' is followed by the remark: 'I hate a man who
is ashamed of his faith.' In this respect 'The Conversion of St
Wilfrid' anticipates later stories, such as 'The Church that was at
Antioch' (*LR*) and 'The Manner of Men' (*LR*) in which conflicting religious beliefs, shipwreck and conversion are re-examined in
the light of the adventures of St Paul. 'The Conversion of St
Wilfrid' also anticipates stories such as 'The Dog Hervey' and
'The Woman in his Life' in which animals become the instru-
ments of spiritual healing and salvation.

But in 'The Conversion of St Wilfrid' there is no complacency
in the picture of Meon's conversion and in the endorsement of a
broader spiritual sense and a generosity of spirit. That picture
and that approval do not accommodate all the forces at play in the
text. Throughout the story there is an implicit criticism – a sense
of something unsatisfactory in an institutionalized Christianity
that fails to take sufficient account of darker and despairing impulses. So in 'The Conversion of St Wilfrid' the triumph of
Meon's conversion to Christianity is undermined by St Wilfrid's
hesitancy, his confused and troubled retrospection, and his unexplained suicidal impulses throughout the story. 'I fear I must
have been a trouble to my friends', he says, and an atmosphere of
gentle sadness suffuses the tale, counterpointed with images of
sorrow and death. Jimmy, the carpenter's son, is in tears; there is
mention of 'old graves' and the 'empty Church', and when Sam

pounds on the bell it emits a 'hollow groaning boom'. St Wilfrid seems to find no outlet in his religion for his doubts and fear, and is an isolated figure. By contrast, the pagan god acknowledges and accommodates his peoples' dark experiences, and St Wilfrid's account of pagan customs reveal his own predilections:

'Why did they kill themselves?' Una asked.

'Because they were heathen. When they grew tired of life (as if *they* were the only people!) they would jump into the sea. They called it going to Wotan. It wasn't want of food always – by any means. A man would tell you he felt grey in the heart, or a woman would say that she saw nothing but long days in front of her; and they saunter away to the mud flats, and – that would be the end of them.'

Here the self-pitying parenthesis points to St Wilfrid's partly repressed despair, and recalls other characters in the earliest stories who were also unable to find in Christianity the strength for endurance, as, for example, in 'The Judgement of Dungara':

Few Pastors will tell you of these things any more than they will speak of that young David of St Bees who, set apart for the Lord's work, broke down in utter desolation and returned half-distraught to the Head Mission, crying, 'There is no God, but I have walked with the Devil!'

These dark psychic energies are related to the political (and psychological) imperialism of some of the earlier stories. It is as if insistence on the control of the outer world becomes a salve to inner despair. The attempt to manage negativity on its own terms leads Kipling to absolutism and a crude philosophy of action. Here the rhetoric of the Old Testament (and of Islam) is especially important. From *Plain Tales from the Hills* to *Puck of Pook's Hill* the highly codified socio-religious polity, the fear of an angry and irrational god, and the system of brutal justice that Kipling found and admired in the Old Testament is reflected in his correspond-ing love of Islam. 'The Old Testament served Kipling as an armoury of grim instances and menacing visions to drive home the imperial code; or, on occasions when the imperial masters failed to live up to this code, of scorching rhetorical language (though more of malignancy than grandeur) for the chastisement of a generation of vipers', wrote Edmund Wilson in 1923 (p. 162). For this reason the protagonists of many of the stories up to *Rewards and Fairies* bypass Christianity and offer in its place a life of work and fellowship. It is a man's work, rather than any kind of doctrinal belief that keeps the forces of evil – pain, fear and moral collapse – at bay. Alan Sandison suggests that in these stories the presentation of Empire becomes a metaphor for the tensions of a moral universe in which man works in confederacy with others against dark, terrifying shapes that threaten him. Those who survive do so by immersing themselves in their work, building and defending structures in order to appropriate something of their substance and pattern (1964, pp. 146–67). Kipling introduces 'The Story of Aurelian McGoggin' (*PTH*) with the statement 'This is not a tale exactly . . . [It] is a Feat.' And the same notion may have inspired the writer of an unsigned review of *Life's Handicap* who wrote: 'It is idle to call these marvellous glimpses into a strange life stories in the ordinary sense of the word – they are revelations of what man can do' (*Edinburgh Monthly Magazine*, 1891, p. 732). 'All art is one, man – one!' says Hal O' the Draft in 'The Wrong Thing'. Thus Mr Springett's Village Hall and Findlayson's Bridge will be '*pukka* – permanent – to endure when all memory of the builder has perished', and in *The Light that Failed*, Dick Heldar does not speak glibly when he says 'My work is everything I have, am or hope to be.' In March 1890 Kipling wrote to E. Kay Robinson:

> Least of all can a man do aught if he think about it, and tries to add cubits to his stature, mental or physical . . . his business is to think as little about his soul as possible for that breeds self-consciousness and loss of power . . . It's an awful thing to think that each Soul has to work out its own salvation and more awful to think that if it sits down to think about that salvation, it is in deep danger of losing it. (Birkenhead, 1980, pp. 125–6)

As one contemporary reviewer put it: 'Mr Kipling is of the aggressive British type whose sermons are told in action alone' (*Harper's Bazaar*, 1901, p. 797).

Increasingly in Kipling's writing, however, the code of action proves inadequate to the burden of experience, and the stories strain against the structures and ethic in which they are enclosed. A transition is registered in the later children's tales. In *Puck of Pook's Hill* Parnesius tells the story of 'The Winged Hats' in an unfamiliar part of the woods. 'This is sadder and darker than the Voltaerrae end', the narrator explains; and in *Rewards and Fairies*, during Sir Richard's terrible narration of the death of Harold in 'The Tree of Justice', Dan shivers and says: 'I think this tale is getting like the woods . . . darker and twistier every minute.'

In the last three collections of stories the treatment of Christianity becomes more sympathetic. The emphasis is now upon suffering rather than repression, the New Testament rather than the Old. Here, the fictional transformation of scenes and incidents from the Gospels, the Acts of the Apostles and the Epistles of St Paul in the context of the First World War still strongly suggests intolerable pain and suffering. But now the potentially angry and punitive Deity is closely shadowed by 'Marvellous mercies and infinite love'.

The first evidence of Kipling's growing predilection for the New Testament is to be found in 'On the Gate', a story that explores the implications of war from a 'Divine' point of view. The narrative takes the form of a conversation between Azrael, the angel of Death, and St Peter, as they supervise 'volunteer staff' laid on to deal with the sudden emergency. 'We are dying in a new age', Azrael tells St Peter, and the administration of Heaven can no longer cope with 'the incoming multitude of all races, tongues and creeds' seeking admission at its gates:

> So many pore ladies and gentlemen, sir, 'oo might well 'ave lived another few years, goin' off, as you might say, in every direction with no time for the proper obsequities.

Contrary to what one might expect in 'A tale of '16', the main emphasis is upon forgiveness and redemption (although no Germans are admitted to Kipling's heaven). All forms of 'judgement' and 'punishment' are alien to Heaven's enterprise:

> He turned to a prim-lipped Seraph who had followed him

with an expulsion-form for signature. St Peter glanced it
over. 'Private R. M. Buckland,' he read, 'on the charge of
saying that there is no God. That all?'

'He says he is prepared to prove it, sir, and – according to
the Rules –'

'If you will make yourself acquainted with the Rules,
you'll find they lay down that "the fool says in his heart,
there is no God." That decides it; probably shell-shock . . .
Pass him in at once!'

Intent upon exploring the mystery of Divine grace, Kipling
abandons his earlier criticism of particular Christian denomi-
nations: in this story Bradlaugh, Bunyan and Calvin join forces as
'pickets' at the gates of Hell. Judas Iscariot and Mary Magdalene
are also enlisted in the cause: they work with St Christopher, St
Paul and St Luke along the 'convoy' guiding weak souls past 'the
voluble and insinuating spirits who strove to draw them aside'.
But supervising all, 'on the Gate twenty-two hours out of the
twenty-four', is St Peter himself who, because of his own betrayal
of Christ, most fully comprehends the need for absolute compassion: 'Oh, my child, *you* don't know what it is to need forgiveness. Be gentle with 'em – be very gentle with 'em!' Every soul
that is safely admitted into Heaven demonstrates the extent of
Divine mercy. Even the 'Deserter; Spy; Murderer', whose case
nearly defeats St Peter is saved by the recollection of God's word:
'Samuel Two, Double Fourteen . . . "*Yet doth He devise means . . .
that His banished be not expelled from Him*!"' Such is the force of these
words that Satan himself – 'that only one of all created beings who
is doomed to perish utterly' – can take comfort from them and
feels able to hope for mercy at the end.

Throughout the story the mystery of forgiveness and acceptance
is conveyed through elements of the comic and the mock-heroic.
One of the most moving descriptions is St Peter's assessment of
St Christopher: 'St Christopher, of course, will pass anything that
looks wet and muddy.' In a parody of Civil Service bureaucracy,
no souls are admitted to Heaven until they have been interviewed
by the 'Assessors on the Board of Admission', and until the
appropriate form has been filled in and checked:

The Seraph handed him a vivid scarlet document. 'The next time,' said St Peter, folding it down and writing on one corner, 'that you get one of these – er – tinted forms, mark it QMA and pass bearer at once.'

An old lady, firmly clutching a mottle-nosed, middle-aged Major by the belt, pushed across a procession of keen-faced *Poilus*, and blocked his path

'I found him! I've got him! Pass him!' she ordered. St Peter's jaw fell. Death politely looked elsewhere. 'There are a few formalities,' the Saint began.

St Peter glanced at the agonised Major and hastily in-itialled him a pass.

Heaven itself is humorously presented as an enormous Office of Death with prefabricated temporary structures to deal with the extra demand, and advance warning of each death is transmitted via SOS signals on a wireless installation with less than perfect reception: 'Waves are always jamming here', a Seraph says. While St Peter and Azrael embark on an inter-departmental inspection, 'Normal Civil Death, KG, KT, KP, PC' complains about having to 'give up two-thirds of my Archives basement (E.7–E.64) to the Polish Civilian Casualty Check and Audit . . . And they've just been cross-indexed, too'.

The narrative also mocks the language and figures of conventional religion, but at times the delicate and tender word-play is strangely moving:

'Which Department is QMA?' said Death. St Peter chuckled. 'It's not a department. It's a Ruling. "*Quia multum amavit.*" A most useful Ruling.'
'Good!' St Peter rubbed his hands. 'That brings her under the higher allowance – GLH scale – "Greater love hath no man – "'
The shift trooped on – such an array of Powers, Honours, Glories, Toils, Patiences, Services, Faiths and Loves as no man can conceive even by favour of dreams.

Perhaps most interesting of all, is the story's portrayal of the 'high' figures of Western religious tradition as ordinary people. St Ignatius Loyola is 'an officer and a gentleman to boot'; St Paul is a problem-case who needs praise and special handling: 'Perhaps . . . a well-timed reference to his seamanship in the Mediterranean'; Judas Iscariot is volatile and oriental: 'This way, please. Many mansions, gentlemen! Go-od billets! Don't you notice these low people, Sar'; and the saints and angels are presented in their human aspect: exhausted, overworked and subjected to extreme pressures and strains:

> A Seraph entered and dropped, panting, on a form. His plumage was ragged, his sword splintered to the hilt; and his face still worked with the passions of the world he had left, as his soiled vesture reeked of alcohol.
>
> 'Defeat,' he reported hoarsely
>
> 'So? We try again,' said the impassive Chief Seraph
>
> 'It's so difficult, though,' a soft-eyed Patience whispered. 'I fail again and again.'

On the one hand, as J. M. S. Tompkins suggests, the story demonstrates that there is enough hell on earth to suspend the notion of retribution: 'What further payment should be exacted from those who were muddy and wet and did not desert?' (1959, p. 212). On the other hand, the story also seeks to locate religion firmly in the world of ordinary reality, which, though painful, has its own supports, as the accompanying poem indicates:

> *But the everyday world of business, meals, and clothing*
> *Builds a bulkhead 'twixt Despair and the Edge of Nothing.*

'The Church that was at Antioch' and 'The Manner of Men', too, explore the lives and problems of spiritual figures in the context of the working lives of the active men of the world. Kipling ingeniously uses the hints in the New Testament to create the characters of the disciples Peter and Paul, but the events of their lives are imaginatively framed by the concerns and preoccupations of the Roman soldiers and the Spanish and Sidonian sailors who narrate the tales. In the foreground of 'The Church that was at Antioch' is Lucius Sergius, Roman Prefect, whose attitude to

Christianity is entirely pragmatic: 'My objection to fancy religions is that they mostly meet after dark, and that means more work for the Police.' And in 'The Manner of Men' the famous shipwreck of Acts 20 is retold 'sailor-fashion' by the Sidonians Sulinor and Quabil: 'Quabil began to illustrate his voyage with date and olive stones from the table . . . Their talk ran professionally.' Such is the emphasis on the 'real' in this story that even the epigraph is literal: Paul *has* actually 'fought with beasts' (I Corinthians 15.32); 'Did *you* ever see his back?' Sulinor asks.[6]

'The Manner of Men' is a striking portrait of Paul. Quabil describes his courage and forcefulness: 'he seemed to take it for granted that he led everywhere . . . he did not know fear.' But the events of the narrative show how Paul's power really lies in the way he has adapted himself to 'the manner of men' and impresses himself on them so that he lives in their memories and thoughts. This is particularly evident if the story is read alongside the biblical narrative: Acts 20 focuses on Paul as the 'hero' of the tale, but Kipling's version sees him only as he affects others: 'all things to all men'. Here the emphasis is upon the disciple trying to sub-jugate his powerful ego to the service of God by entering the lives of others. 'I am so poor a soul that I flinch from touching dead pig', he tells Sulinor, who is sensitive to his inner struggles and self-contempt: 'You seem to have both ends and the bight of most things coiled down in your little head, Paul.' But Kipling centres the narrative on the men Paul is affecting without their fully realizing or acknowledging it. What emerges is Paul's imaginative tact. He sees each man as he is: 'he had the woman's trick of taking the tone and colour of whoever he talked to'. He handles Quabil's touchiness, Sulinor's silent fear of the beasts, and the prisoners on board the ship precisely as each requires:

When he saw that trying to – er – cheer me made me angry, he dropped it. Like a woman again.

He knew! Fire – sword – the sea – torture even – one does not think of them too often. But not the Beasts! Aie! *Not* the Beasts!

'Paul went down and told them there was no danger and

they believed him! . . . He asked me for the keys of the leg-bars to make them easier. "*I've* been through this sort of thing before," he said, "but they are new to it down below. Give me the keys." I told him there was no order for him to have any keys: . . . He looked at me like an old gull lounging just astern of one's taffrail in a full gale. *You* know that eye, Spaniard!'

The effect is paradoxical. The narrative suggests that in some sense the lives and characters of the sailors have not been changed by their experience of Paul. Even as he tells the story Quabil expresses his dislike and dismisses him: 'Mad! Mad as a magician on market-day'; 'Too much muttering and laying-on of hands for *me*.' Sulinor is more sympathetic yet despite his long conversations with Paul and Paul's humble service to him ('he . . . washed me clean after dysentery'), he is not a convert to Christianity. At the same time, however, the outcome of the story suggests that Paul affected them each in their own way by contributing to a deepening of their sense of life. Quabil befriends the young Spanish captain who reminds him of his dead son: 'He was rather like you about the eyes'; and Sulinor joins the Roman fleet: 'Five – four years ago I might have been waiting for you anywhere in the Long Puddle with fifty River men – and no moon.' In each case their action seems to result from their experience of Paul: he met them on their own terms, helped them and served them:

> When I was getting better, and Paul was washing me off once, he asked me if my citizenship were in order . . . Well it was and it was not . . . And Paul said to me: 'Serve Caesar . . . If you serve Caesar . . . you will be at least obeying some sort of law.'

In this story, self is not lost in religious ecstasy as it is in some of the earlier Indian stories, but in imaginative identifications with the ordinary lives of other men. In this respect the poem that follows the story is deeply moving, for as a prayer to Christ it expresses in human terms the fact that for Paul 'reward' would be restoration to 'himself' after a lifetime of self-sacrifice for Christ's sake:

Since I was overcome
　By that great Light and Word,
I have forgot or forgone
The self men call their own
(Being made all things to all men)
　So that I might save some
　At such small price, to the Lord,
As being all things to all men.

I was made all things to all men,
But now my course is done –
And now is my reward –
Ah, Christ, when I stand at Thy Throne
With those I have drawn to the Lord,
Restore me to my self again!

'The Church that was at Antioch' picks up and develops the theme of the problems of discipleship already hinted at in 'The Manner of Men'. The story's epigraph is taken from Galatians 2.11 – 'But when Peter was come to Antioch, I withstood him to the face, because he was to blame' – and refers to the arguments of the early Church over whether Jews and Gentiles should eat at the same table. The concluding poem, 'The Disciple', contains a warning to Peter, Paul and all 'disciples' that every disciple has his limitations of vision and his own personality is a potential threat to truth. There is an obvious analogy with the chameleon ambivalence of the artist:

It is His Disciple
　(Ere Those Bones are dust)
Who shall change the Charter,
　Who shall split the Trust –
Amplify distinctions,
　Rationalise the Claim,
Preaching that the Master
　Would have done the same

　　　　.　　.　　.　　.

He that hath a Gospel
　Whereby Heaven is won

> (Carpenter, or Cameleer,
>   Or Maya's dreaming son),
> Many swords shall pierce Him,
>   Mingling blood with gall;
> But His Own Disciple
>   Shall wound Him worst of all!

In this story the contrast between Peter's brooding nature and Paul's energetic and articulate vision is very powerful. Paul is presented sympathetically as a radical thinker who is *struggling* to understand Christ's vision, to live in accordance with and to guide the early Church. His first conversation with Valens reveals that he has not yet mastered his pride:

> 'I expect you march in heavier order than I.'
> 'What would you call your best day's work?' Valens asked in turn.
> 'I have covered . . .' Paulus checked himself. 'And yet not I but the God,' he muttered. 'It's hard to cure oneself of boasting.'

But, appropriately for the Paul of Acts and Galatians, who strove to free Christianity from the constraints of the Law, he is more immediately sympathetic than Peter to the claims of 'spirit' over 'law', and can respond at once to what Valens says about God changing men's hearts rather than making laws:

> 'As a servant of Mithras, I eat with any initiate, so long as the food is clean,' said Valens.
>   'But,' said Petrus, '*that* is the crux.'
>   'Mithras also tells us,' Valens went on, 'to share a bone covered with dirt, if better cannot be found.'
>   'You observe no difference, then, between peoples at your feasts?' Paulus demanded.
>   'How dare we? We are all his children. Men make laws. Not Gods,' Valens quoted from the Old Ritual . . . 'Gods do not make laws. They change men's hearts. The rest is the Spirit.'

Peter, on the other hand, is uncertain about the food laws: 'It is true that I have eaten with Gentiles – Yet, at the time, I doubted if it were wise.' But it is he, not Paul, who intuitively realizes that there is no need to baptise Valens as he lies dying: 'Think you that one who has spoken Those Words needs such as *we* to certify him to any God?' His belief that this would be merely convention, set alongside the references to Mithraism in the story and to 'Maya's dreaming son' in the accompanying poem, suggests that Kipling retained his conviction that no single religion has the monopoly of truth. The conversation of Valens with his uncle at the beginning of the story restates his belief that there are the same archetypes within different religions, called by different names, and that the same basic patterns underlie all doctrine and religious observance:

> 'We've a College here of stiff-necked Hebrews who call themselves Christians.'
> 'I've heard of them,' said Valens. 'There isn't a ceremony or symbol they haven't stolen from the Mithras ritual.'
>
> 'Even these Christians are divided now. You see . . . one part of their worship is to eat together.'
> 'Another theft! The Supper *is* the essential Symbol with us,' Valens interrupted.

At the end of the story Valens himself can be seen as a Christ figure. Stabbed to death in a dark alley by a coward who uses a child as a decoy, Valens repeatedly begs mercy for his murderers. His words recall those of the dying Christ on the cross: 'The Cilician and his friends . . . Don't be hard on them . . . They get worked up . . . They don't know what they are doing'. Here too the references to his 'concubine' recall Christ's love and compassion for Mary Magdalene. In this context, however, the language suggests that a sacrificial human love is divine, if anything is, and that the one is best understood in terms of the other. At the same time, there is no easy interchange between the human and the supernatural in the story. In a final narrative twist, Peter and Paul are seen to be subservient to Valens, they are not the 'heroes' of this story, but only disciples after all.

Notes

1   *London Quarterly Review*, October 1893, p. 185. See also the *Academy*, October 1891, p. 327; *Athenaeum*, August 1890, p. 279; *Bookman*, July 1893, p. 111.

2   For biographical information concerning Kipling's parents see Baldwin (1960).

3   *Proofs of Holy Writ* was first published in the *Strand Magazine*, April 1934.

4   (Weygandt, 1939, pp. 159–60.) See also Gibbs (1925, p. 32): 'One must know not only such generally known characters as Saul, Samson, Joseph, Uriah and Noah . . . but also little known characters like Naboth, Lemuel, Boaz, Tubal-Cain, Hiram Alitt, Jubal and others. For Kipling's biblical allusions see also Gribbon (1954); MacMunn (1934) and Colvin (1938).

5   For Kipling and Christian missions see Gilbert (1986).

6   That Paul *literally* 'fought with beasts' is Kipling's own version of the story: there is no evidence in the Bible for this. See Dummelow (1909, p. 919): '*I have fought with beasts*: probably a metaphor for some plot of the Jews or attack of the mob. His Roman citizenship and influential friends would have saved him from actually having to fight wild beasts in the theatre; and this, if it had really happened, would probably have been specially mentioned.'

6

'Nothing is left except the words':
The redefinition of fantasy

In a poem at the end of *Actions and Reactions* Kipling wrote:

> Our loves, our tears, as water
>   Are spilled upon the ground
> God giveth no man quarter,
>   Yet God a means hath found,
> Though Faith and Hope have vanished,
>   And even love grows dim –
> A means whereby His banished
>   Be not expelled from Him!

Another of Kipling's hidden narratives is his rewriting of Christian motifs. Here, as he reimagines intercessionary or mediatory figures, 'the edges or ends of inconceivable experiences' are as sharply present as in the early stories. But now the uncanny enlarges our sense of the peculiarly human. Its restorative energies are not transcendental. Systems of thought and belief, positing spiritual absolutes, are guaranteed no objective foundation; but the figures of redemption they generate retain a magical potency.

As early as 'The Children of the Zodiac' (*MI*) Kipling had written of the healing powers of the artist and his or her self-sacrifice in the service of others. In this story the artist (song-writer) devotes his life to others and sacrifices his divinity on their behalf. The main emphasis of the story falls on the contrast between the old man at the beginning of the story who runs away from the Archer's arrow, and his counterpart at the end who 'stood still waiting till the arrow struck':

'I die,' he said quietly. 'It is well for me, Leo, that you sang for forty years . . . I should have run away but for your songs. My work is done, and I die without making a great show of my fear.'

Elsewhere, however, the emphasis is upon figures whose burden of suffering and self-sacrifice more closely resembles that of Christ, and who derive their symbolism from the Bible and from medieval romance. In *Puck of Pook's Hill* Hugh is described as the type of suffering and love: 'the most perfect, courteous, valiant, tender and wise knight that ever drew breath'. In *Rewards and Fairies* there are two stories – 'Cold Iron' and 'The Knife and the Naked Chalk' – which explicitly compare the curative power of artistic and religious 'experience'. In these stories we have a modification of the heroic attitude and a complex reassessment of dream. 'Cold Iron' and 'The Knife and the Naked Chalk' carry a suggestion that dream-life is a false fabrication, seductive but worth less than ordinary waking consciousness. An explicit acknowledgement of 'the teeth of the beast in your own heart' is linked with the need for mediating figures. There is however, no straightforward moral at stake. For if, as the Flint Man discovers in 'The Knife and the Naked Chalk', the enemy within is such that it 'can affect and corrupt and finally destroy the spirit of the gods'; and if, as Hal discovers in 'The Wrong Thing', art is not produced in egotistic frenzy, 'all in a heat after supper', then the self-forgetting, plural voices of the narrative are all the more necessary to it. In these stories, the narrative still emphasizes secrecy and disguise. From *Puck of Pook's Hill* to *Limits and Renewals* the stories suggest that initiation into new states of consciousness is outside the control of the artist – a 'mad humour' – and could exact a heavy price: 'I do not know whether I shall return in my own shape', the Flint Man in 'The Knife and the Naked Chalk' tells us.

In 'Cold Iron' Kipling makes an explicit comparison between 'the Boy's' loss of his magic powers and Christ's human incarnation: 'Iron out of Calvary is master of men all.' In this story the Boy's 'Magic' has a power and an unearthly beauty that enthralls the fairy people who adopted him:

There was flash on flash against the clouds, and rush on rush of shadows down the valley till the shaws were full of hounds giving tongue, and the woodways were packed with his knights in armour riding down into the water-mists . . . Behind them you could see great castles lifting slow and splendid on arches of moonshine, with maidens waving their hands at the windows

But Puck realizes that the 'shadow-nights and shadow-girls' are merely a distraction: 'I saw him lift his eyes . . . towards folk in housen all the time . . . his heart aching to go straightforward among [them].' The 'Cold Iron' which the Boy must avoid if he is to retain his magical powers represents the sorrow and suffering inseparable from the human condition. 'What could you or I have done against the Smith that made it and laid it for him to find?' Puck asks Sir Huon. And like Leo in 'The Children of the Zodiac', the Boy sees it as his mission to go among 'folk in housen' and alleviate their sorrow as best he can. The runes on the slave-ring he fastens round his neck as a symbol of his servitude signify the mystery of faith: 'Few can see / Further forth', and his intuitive but uncomprehending acceptance of his fate confirms Puck's confident assertion at the opening of the story: 'Where there's true faith, there's no call for magic.' In 'Cold Iron' the diminishment of fantasy – 'a fag end of a charm here, or half spell there' – transforms a fairy story into a variant of the Fall motif.

In 'The Knife and the Naked Chalk' the sacrifice of the Flint Man is also described in the language and imagery of the Bible: 'It was for the sheep. The sheep are the people . . . What else could I have done?' His anguished solitude and fear both before and after the putting out of his right eye resemble Christ's in the Garden of Gethsemane. 'O poor – poor God', says Puck as the Flint Man describes the effects of his sacrifice:

I warm myself and eat at any fire I choose, but there is no *one* to light me a fire or cook my meat. I sold all that when I bought the Magic Knife for my people . . . and I knew that they thought me to be a God, like the God Tyr, who gave his right hand to conquer a great beast . . . My heart grew little

and cold; a wind shouted in my ears, my eye darkened, I
said to my Mother, 'Can a God die?' . . . and I fell into
darkness full of hammer noises.

But this story, like 'Cold Iron', is evasive as well as allusive and
the intricacy of its surface again reveals Kipling's preference for
open rather than closed narrative forms; in each instance any
merely straightforward allegorical equivalence would be reductive. The story concerns not just the act of self-sacrifice, but
the dangers and difficulties involved along the way: 'the Beast' is
more than a physical threat – inside as well as out, it also
represents the potential wholesale destruction of social meaning
and identity. We use language to repel the Beast to escape from
the demands of the unconscious. In 'The Knife and the Naked
Chalk', evocative juxtapositions and unusual applications of
words alert the reader to a powerful unifying device; different
names describe the same thing. The Flint Man is alternately 'the
Son of the Priestess', 'The Buyer of the Knife' and 'The Keeper
of the People'; and the wolf is variously described as, 'The Curse
of the Chalk', 'Grey Shepherd', 'Fleet in the Night' and 'The
Beast'. This note is introduced by Una at the very beginning
when she says:

> [Mr Dudeney] did not talk like their own people in the
> Weald of Sussex, and he used different names for farm
> things, but he understood how they felt and let them go with
> him.

However, through the Flint Man's encounters with the Children
of the Night, the narrative also points to the misuse and mis-
appropriation of words, and to their ultimate emptiness. The
Flint Man himself introduces the episode in the woods with the
graphic image of being transformed into 'talking water', and the
nightmarish, hallucinatory qualities of his journey are all described in terms of language:

> I was made to sing songs and to mock the Trees, though
> I was afraid of them. At the same time I saw myself laugh-
> ing, and I was very sad for this fine young man who was
> myself

I wished to speak to these men, but the words were changed in my mouth, and all I could say was, 'Do not make that noise. It hurts' . . They changed my words between my teeth till I wept.

Even when he believes he has regained control of his senses the trance-like quality of his description makes us suspicious: 'I spoke many words that went smoothly along like sheep in order.' And when he returns to his own people the confusion continues:

they began to sing a song in the Old Tongue – *The Song of Tyr*. I sang with them, but my Mother's brother said, 'This is *your* song, O Buyer of the knife. Let *us* sing it, Tyr.' Even then I did not understand, till I saw that – that no man stepped on my shadow; and I knew that they thought me to be a God, like the God Tyr, who gave his right hand to conquer a Great Beast . . . I was afraid. I said to myself, 'My Mother and my Maiden will know I am not Tyr.' But *still* I was afraid, with the fear of a man who falls into a steep flint-pit while he runs, and feels that it will be hard to climb out.

The end of the story confirms the Flint Man's initial statement that 'one cannot feed some things on names and songs': 'Nothing is left except the words and the songs, and the worship of a God. I would sell them all', he says. As in 'Cold Iron', where Puck explains to the reader that it was the Boy's 'own dear self and not the words worked the wonder', so in this story there is the sense that something more than the words and the songs are needed to sustain the fading spirit. Leo's sacrifice in 'The Children of the Zodiac' is no longer enough. In her compassion and her steadfast acceptance of him as he is, the mediatory role played by the Flint Man's mother in 'The Knife and the Naked Chalk' anticipates the women in the late stories, who seem to personify a state of grace:

She knew. As soon as I dropped she knew. When my spirit came back I heard her whisper in my ear, 'Whether you live or die, or are made different, I am your Mother.' That was good – better even than the water she gave me and the going away of the sickness. Though I was ashamed to have fallen down, yet I was very glad.

In 'The Tender Achilles' (*LR*) and 'Unprofessional' (*LR*) the mediatory figures are shaped by visionary notions of healing. Kipling had always been interested in doctors. The 'most business-like visitor' of 'Baa Baa, Black Sheep' who rescues Punch from the House of Desolation is a doctor. In *Rewards and Fairies* 'Marklake Witches' and 'A Doctor of Medicine' are structured around Laennec, inventor of the stethoscope, and the herbalist and astrologer Culpeper. Fictional doctors – Sir John Chartres, Dr L. Rutherford Gilbert, Sir James Belton, Sir Thomas Horringe and Keede – are also accorded a place of honour in the late stories. Here Kipling develops the idea explored through the experiences of the mythical characters in *Rewards and Fairies* – the need for the strong and the respected to recognize their own limitations. His notion of 'the healing art' recalls the archetypal figure of the wounded healer: the idea of the physician healed through his own suffering, and of the wound that would not heal as the source of curative power.

'The Tender Achilles', like the shell-shock stories explored in chapter 4, concerns delayed reaction to the war: 'Everything that a man's brain automatically shoves into the background was out before the footlights.' For Wilkett 'this Hell's hoop-la' is prompted by guilt at the deaths of those he had been unable to save because of the impossible demands made on doctors at the front line:

> He said there was blood on everything that he ate. He said he's been guilty of the murder of a certain number of men because he hadn't operated on 'em properly. He had their names down in a pocket-book. He said he might have saved 'em if he hadn't knocked off for a cigarette or a doss . . . He saw perspectives of heads – gunshot wounds seen from above and a little behind, as they'd lie on the tables; . . . but still they accused him of murder.

Wilkett also nurses a foot injury which acts both as a 'safety-valve' for his mental anguish and, as he believes, 'a judgement on him for shirking'. We measure his exaggerated sense of duty and self-expectation in the response of his colleagues:

> I told him we were all alike, and the conditions of our job hadn't been human. I said there were limits to the machine. We'd been forced to go beyond 'em, and we ought to be thankful we'd been able to do as much as we had. Then he wrung his hands and said, 'Where much has been given to a fellow much being required.' That annoyed me. I hate book-keeping with God! It's dam' insolence anyhow. Who was he to know how much had been given to the other fellow?

Even Sir James Belton, Head of St Peggotty's, speaks in terms of reasonable expectations: 'Gen-tel-men. In our Pro-fession we are none of us Jee-ho-vahs.' For Keede and Sir Thomas Horringe too, pain and suffering are a part of strength: 'You've got to acknowledge the facts of life and your own limitations.' Their good-humoured banter and light-hearted anecdotes about surgical exploits during the war do in fact reveal their pride in what, in spite of all, they managed to achieve:

> 'But God is great as they say in Mespot. Sometimes you get a card from the base saying you didn't stitch his diaphragm to his larynx and he's doing well. There was a machine-gunner . . . I *must* have left the bloke his stomach, but I fancy I made a clean sweep of everything below the duodenum. And now he's a head-gardener near Plaxtol. Pinches his employer's celery and sends it to me in sugar-boxes.'
>
> This reminded Scree of a man one-third of whose brain he had personally removed, who on recovery wished to show his gratitude by becoming his Town Chauffeur.

At the end of the story Wilkett's cure is effected by means of a deliberate 'mistake' on the part of his colleagues. In spite of the unlimited resources at St Peggotty's, they operate on an incorrect diagnosis and then dismiss the 'little affair' as all in a day's work. Wilkett reacts precisely as they had anticipated: 'But you had all the *time* you wanted! You had no reason to *hurry*! You were under no *strain*! You had only to label and number.' When, however, they pretend to accuse each other of the error of judgement and it begins to look as if jobs will be lost, Wilkett displays some saving graces, 'apologising at last'. But to the very end of the story he remains offensive and unlikeable. His 'physical' cure does not extend to his moral or imaginative self and he could be the speaker in the epigraph to the story who 'cast away . . . That lone star . . . Furthest, but most faithful' through self-love.

In 1908 Kipling's address to the medical students of the Middlesex Hospital – 'A Doctor's Work' (1928, pp. 41–7) – showed both his respect for the medical profession in general and his own high moral concept of the doctor's duty. In a speech given at the annual dinner of the Royal College of Surgeons in February 1923, later entitled 'Surgeons and the Soul' (1928, pp. 209–13), he openly expounded his layman's theories about the relation of medical science to psychology, astrology and mysticism. Beginning his address with the legendary Brahminic story of the hiding of man's divinity 'where Man will never dream of looking for it . . . inside Man himself', he went on to speak of man's quest through the ages to relocate it. Arguing that 'the Medicine Man, the Healer' has been 'hottest on its track', he describes the surgeon in terms suggestive of the healing art of Christ:

> Is it any wonder, gentlemen of the College of Surgeons, that your calling should exact the utmost that man can give – full knowledge, exquisite judgement, and skill in the highest, to be put forth, not at any self-chosen moment, but daily at the need of others? More than this. Your dread art demands that instant, impersonal vision which in one breath, one beat of the pulse, can automatically dismiss every preconceived idea and impression, and as automatically recognise, accept, and overcome whatever of new and unsuspected menace may have slid into the light beneath your steadfast hands.
>
> But such virtue is not reached or maintained except by a life's labour, a life's single-minded devotion. (pp. 212–13)

Kipling had previously entertained visionary notions of healing. In *Kim* the Sahiba uses 'the mysterious earth-currents which thrill the clay of our bodies' to cure Kim; and in *Kim* and 'A Doctor of Medicine' Kipling links the conventional sciences with the unorthodox science of astrology. 'In the Same Boat' and 'Fairy Kist', however, suggest that the power of healing is as dependent on imaginative as on scientific processes; and the following exchange between Harries and Loftie in 'Unprofessional' epitomizes the increasing emphasis in the late stories on the role of imagination in science:

> 'Don't think! *Watch!*'
> 'Or imagine?' Loftie supplemented.
> 'You've got it. Imagination *is* what we want. This rigid "thinking" game is hanging up research. You told me yourself, the other night, it was becoming all technique and no advance.'

'Unprofessional' is Kipling's most challenging study of these themes. In this story orthodox medical practice turns Mrs Berners and her sufferings into a number, '128'; and the latest equipment – 'stoves, filters, sterilizers, frigidaria' – does not provide a 'scientific' explanation for the suicidal impulse in the mice and in Mrs Berners herself. Instead, this impulse is described in a way that suggests an imaginative apprehension of the processes of breakdown:

> a characteristic unease, followed by nervous crises – as shown – culminating in what seems to be attempts at suicide . . . as – a house explodes through its own windows under the vacuum set up by a tornado.

J. M. S. Tompkins argues that the suicide motif in this story symbolizes 'the contemporary situation of the human race, strung between the science that can save and a despairing tendency to self-destruction' (1959, p. 171). The very title, 'Unprofessional', points to an ambiguity in the actions and beliefs of the doctors and the uncertain needs of the patient. Its narrative implies a silent recognition of the futility of scientific advance that is accompanied only by human failure and breakdown.

But what is perhaps most striking about the story is the imaginative sympathy felt and expressed for the woman who feels the call of death:

She told them that, when she had nothing to do, she mostly

felt in people's way, and as if she ought to go on elsewhere
. . . She had a trick of tossing her head sideways and up-
wards, sometimes in the midst of her overseeings, and would
say: 'Well, well! I can't keep at this all the time. I must be off
elsewhere where I'm wanted.' . . . 'I don't want to die, Mr
Loftie. But I've *got* to. I've really *got* to get out of this. I'm
wanted elsewhere, but' – she shivered – 'I don't like going.'

Like Yeats, who wrote in 'The Wheel' of the knowledge that
'what stirs our blood / Is but its longing for the tomb', Kipling is
involved here in the exploration of the soul's search for death. Mrs
Berners' words – 'I must be off elsewhere where I'm wanted' –
express a yearning akin to Yeats's, and Kipling's presentation of
her situation seems to point to a radical reassessment of a conventional view of suicide and of death. 'After what you said outside Barker's in the wet, you don't think I *really* want to die, Mr
Frost?' Mrs Berners asks; but the story itself seems to question
whether the expectation and desire for existence is the fundamental emotional force of life, or its fundamental illusion. There
is something compelling about Mrs Berners' perspective: 'I ought
to be busy dying.'

The use of astrology in medical experimentation represents
another creative heresy: 'A man's entitled to use a telescope as
well as a microscope, isn't he?' In 'Unprofessional' the study of
'planetary influences' and the 'tides' they cause in human cells
leads to the discovery of a cure for cancer. In 'The Threshold',
the poem that accompanies the story, the movement from modern/
scientific to primitive/irrational (or the integration of the two) is
reflected in the description of the plural gods of 'Ionia': 'The
Horse, the Elk, and the Bison . . . / The Mammoth, Tiger and
Bear'. Here the implication is that no single image of god accounts for the range of human emotions and experience, and the
description of some of the gods as arbitrary, cruel and unpredict-
able – 'wooed by worship and won by sacrifice' – recalls the role
played by Thor on 'Cold Iron' and the angry gods of the early
Indian stories. In each instance the mysterious power of the
godhead seems to derive from the recognition of *both* love and
hate. Just as 'The Tender Achilles' ends with the team uncertain

whether they will be able to repeat their cure, in 'The Threshold' Ionia remains 'Resolute, unsatisfied' because her 'Gods of Death and Terror' cannot be incorporated into the monotheistic view: 'We dream one matter in all things – / Eternal, changeless, unseen.'

Both 'Unprofessional' and its powerful concluding poem imply that no simple affirmation is possible in a human world so full of suffering and a Divine world so enigmatically unjust. The story shows, above all, the need for imaginative daring in recognizing and caring for the needs of the psyche. Kipling develops this daring in four other stories – 'The Wish House' (*DC*), 'Uncovenanted Mercies' (*LR*), 'A Madonna of the Trenches' (*DC*) and 'The Gardener' (*DC*) – which contain his most radical exploration of a spiritual vision of the redemptive possibilities of love. In each instance the victim (a woman) voluntarily accepts the burden on behalf of someone else, and the impulse to act is given by love.[1] It is also the case, however, that the love is illicit – or, in Kipling's words, 'uncovenanted' – and that the motivating impulse may be seen as heretical.

These four stories accord with other *fin de siècle* fictive explorations of female power. Sandra Gilbert has shown how Rider Haggard's *She* could be regarded as 'a pivot' from the Victorian to 'the modern' (1983a, p. 448). For Gilbert the image of 'a woman, draped and blindfolded, carrying a lighted torch' in Conrad's *Heart of Darkness* is also paradigmatic of:

> the contradictions between power (the torch) and powerlessness (the blindfold) and thus it introduces the idea of the other who has been excluded and dispossessed but who, despite such subordination, exercises a kind of indomitable torchlike power.

In Kipling's *The Light that Failed* Dick Heldar's masterpiece is a painting of 'Melancholia' in the likeness of 'a woman who had known all the sorrow in the world and was laughing at it'. Dick's friend Torpenhow expresses admiration for the painting – 'What a face it is! What eyes, and what insolence!' – but his remarks are not unqualified:

> She's seen the game played out, – I don't think she had a
> good time of it, – and now she doesn't care . . . Dick, there's
> a sort of murderous, viperine suggestion in the poise of the
> head that I don't understand.

Kipling's interest in the subversive female desires at stake here is
analogous to explorations of realms of 'otherness' elsewhere in his
writings. India, the occult, dream, magic, the supernatural are
presented as a threat to the supposed control of the Western
rational mind. In the same way, women are also objectified as
other, allowed only their own peculiar blend of witchcraft and
magic. In 1892, the year after he published *The Light that Failed*,
Kipling discussed the notion of something called 'a woman book'
with the publisher William Heinemann. Three years later he
wrote to Heinemann again saying that he couldn't do the book,
but added 'I dream of doing novels with women in them some
fine day'. Kipling never did publish such a novel, but the late
stories include a significant number narrated by women. The
effect of the First World War, with its new technologies of death,
was to reduce 'heroes' to impotent ciphers. One way to come to
terms with history's reduction of heroism was to adopt a female
voice. As Gilbert has shown, women were the dominant figures in
Britain in the war-years: 'As nurses, as mistresses, as munitions
workers, bus drivers, or soldiers in the "land army", even as
wives and mothers, these formerly subservient creatures began to
loom malevolently larger, until it was possible for a visitor to London to observe in 1918 that "England was a world of women"'
(1983b, p. 425). Gilbert also argues for a possible connection
between the wartime activities of women and the sense of sexual
wounding that haunts so many Modernist texts. In Kipling's case
his late studies of women – particularly 'The Wish House' and
'The Gardener' – are characteristically double-edged. They are
brilliant inward stories of love and the power of love and sexual
conquest. But, as John Bayley points out, they are also potent explorations of the hidden connections between compulsive sexual
love and stress-induced disease (1986, p. 23).

Like 'The Church that was at Antioch' and 'The Manner of
Men', 'The Wish House' brings together the ordinary and the

Divine. Most of the narrative is taken up with the 'back-lookin's' of two women, Mrs Ashcroft and Mrs Fettley. They speak in Sussex dialect and their tale is full of local detail. During the course of the conversation, knowing this will be the last time they meet, for Grace Ashcroft is dying of cancer and Liz Fettley is going blind, each tells a story of illicit and unrequited love. Mrs Fettley speaks first. But Mrs Ashcroft's tale is at once more tragic and more complex. She too has remained passionately in love with a man long after he has tired of her, and when she returned home from London once to find him critically ill, she made a pact with a 'Token' at a 'Wish House' to 'take everythin' bad that's in store for my man, 'Arry Mockler, for love's sake'. This, she explains to her friend, is why he has enjoyed continued good health – 'wonderful fleshed up an' restored back' – whereas she has been continually troubled by a 'Long-standing ulcer' which has now become cancerous. ''Twas *so*. Year in, year out . . . 'e got 'is good from me 'thout knowin' – for years and years', she said triumphantly.

The whole setting of their conversation and the narratives of the past suggest that, within the apparently male-orientated world, it is woman's love and vision and caring which, in secret ways, sustain and support: 'No odds twixt boys now an' forty years back. Take all an' give naught – an' we to put up with it!' 'But don't it lay heavy on ye, sometimes?' her friend replies. Both before and after she visits the Wish House Grace Ashcroft accepts suffering as a part of love and faces it courageously. ''Tis like a tooth', her friend comments. 'It must rage and rugg till it tortures itself quiet.' But she herself knows better: 'I knowed it must go on burnin' till it burned me out', she says. In this way the sudden power of intense feeling is converted into sacrificial passion: her love is purified by the intensity of her pain.

In the poems that preface and conclude the story the emphasis is also upon the strength of women's love and their capacity to bear suffering. 'Late Came the God' describes how 'the God' tries to punish woman for the 'wrong' she has committed, but her suffering miraculously creates a love that is 'Resolute, selfless, divine'. At the end of the poem the situation is reversed and the retributive God is seen as wholly inferior to the woman: 'What is a God beside Woman? Dust and derision.' Love and suffering are also linked in 'Rahere': the eye of love transforms the leper, 'faceless, fingerless, obscene', into something without 'blemish':

> 'Tis a motion of the Spirit that revealeth God to man
> In the shape of love exceeding, which regards not taint or fall,
> Since in perfect love, saith Scripture, can be no excess at all.

In the story itself it is also significant that it is a child's experience of love and selfless caring which inspires the adult's. Mrs Ashcroft has been no paragon of conventional virtue: 'You'll pray no man'll ever deal with you like you've dealed with some', her husband tells her on his death-bed; and at one point in the story she asks Liz Fettley, 'if you'll believe it', and receives the reply: 'I do. I lay you're further off lyin' now than in all your life, Gra'.' But Sophy Ellis shows her how suffering can be a proof of sincerity and ultimately of love. The child's demand for belief and trust in the irrational and the imaginative (the trust in the Wish House) suggests the reappearance of the child-spirit of 'They', now asked to play her part not in the remote and magical 'House Beautiful', but on a council estate.

> 'Oh, Mrs Ashcroft,' she says, stretchin' out 'er liddle thin arms. 'I *do* love ye.' There wasn't any holdin' agin that. I took 'er into me lap an' made much of 'er. 'Is it truly gone?' she says. 'Yes,' I says, 'an' if 'twas you took it away, I'm truly grateful.' ' *'Twas* me,' she says, layin' 'er cheek to mine. 'No one but me knows how.' An' then she said she'd changed me 'eddick for me at a Wish 'Ouse.'

Here the presence of the child is all-revealing. She teaches Grace Ashcroft how to transform egotistical suffering into redemptive love. But, more importantly perhaps, she brings, with her return, echoes of the sensuality – the physical intensity of the kiss in 'They' – strangely absent in these mature love stories of Kipling's later years. Held within and without, she is a powerfully daemonic and positive 'anima' figure.

At the end of the story Grace Ashcroft remains concerned that the pain she has endured will continue to keep Harry alive and in health: 'I don't want no more'n this – *if* de pain is taken into de reckonin'.' But we are never entirely sure of the real motivation for her actions. Unlike the child, her motives are both egotistical and fiercely possessive. Nor do we know whether the incident at the Wish House actually took place or was simply imagined. 'Kipling is far closer to Gogol than to a normal realist or naturalist', notes Randall Jarrell (1980, p. 358). 'In Kipling the pressure of the imagination has forced facts over into the supernatural.' In 'The Wish House' the scenes are told in great detail, but the reader remains uncertain of whether they are as 'real' as they are set up to be (see Roskies, 1982, p. 14). Like the woman in 'Late Came the God', 'alone without hope of regard or reward', but 'uncowed', emotions of pity or apology are irrelevant to Grace Ashcroft's situation.

Suffering is also seen to be essential to love and vision in 'Uncovenanted Mercies', but unlike 'The Wish House', where the emphasis is upon carrying physical pain for another, this story is concerned with mental anguish. The action takes place in Hell, which is imaged as a railway station where people wait through eternity for friends and loved ones who never arrive:

A train came in. Porters cried the number of its platform; many of the crowd grouped by the barriers, but some stood fast under the clock, men straightening their ties and women tweaking their hats. An elderly female with a string-bag observed to a stranger: '*I* always think it's best to stay where you promised you would. Less chance o' missing 'im that way.' 'Oh, quite,' the other answered. 'That's what *I* always do'; and then both moved towards the barrier as though drawn by cords.

The passengers filed out – they and the waiting crowd devouring each other with their eyes. Some, misled by a likeness or a half-heard voice, hurried forward crying a name or even stretching out their arms. To cover their error, they would pretend they had made no sign and bury themselves in their uninterested neighbours. As the last passenger came away, a little moan rose from the assembly.

Another train was called. The crowd moved over – some

hopeful in step and bearing; others upheld only by desperate will.

In this dark place, 'the absolute Zeroes of night and silence', Job's sufferings are seen as *passé*, and such is the agony of waiting that Satan, Gabriel and Azrael are overwhelmed by a new and more terrible 'Horror of Great Darkness':

> dimming, first, the lustre of their pinions; bowing, next, their shoulders as the motes in the never-shifted sunbeam filtered through it and settled on them, masking, finally, the radiance of Robe, Sword and very Halo, till only their eyes had light.
>
> The groan broke first from Azrael's lips. 'How long?' he muttered. 'How long?'

In such a place Christ's cry, 'My God! My God! Why hast thou forsaken me?' is seen as the ultimate betrayal, giving rise to the deepest experience of despair, and this overwhelming fear of betrayal is exacerbated by isolation and repeated disappointment: 'We work on hope deferred now', says Satan, 'It acts more certainly . . . The processes are largely mental.'[2] The story concerns the lives and sufferings of a man and a woman who defy the laws of fate and chance in order to meet and consummate their love. As in 'The Wish House', the emphasis is upon the strength and power of the woman. The whole of her being yearns to be with Dick, to give herself to him 'mistress-wise', as the concluding poem puts it, and she suffers paranoid fantasies of being killed before she can meet him:

> 'Just a little lay down and a nice cup of tea' . . . the nurse cooed.
>
> 'Tea? How do I know it won't be poisoned. It *will* be poisoned – I know it will. Let me go! I'll tell the police if you don't let me go! I'll tell – I'll tell! Oh God! – who can I tell?'

By contrast the man is more fearful and for a moment hesitates on the edge of accepting oblivion:

> The man had been brought to with brandy and sal volatile. As he recovered consciousness he groaned.

'I remember now,' said he.

'You needn't;' the doctor spoke slowly. 'We can take away your memory – '

'If I please?' the man stammered.

'Yes. If you authorise me,' the doctor went on.

'Then what becomes of *me*?'

'You'll be free from that pain at any rate. Do you author-ise me?'

'I do not. I'll see you damned first.'

Aware that suffering and self-consciousness are essential to life, he answers the false doctor with courage, but he quickly loses direction again, blundering off towards renewed fear and despair. His plight is echoed in the concluding poem, 'Azrael's Count', where the shifting attitudes of men are contrasted first with the love of a cow for her calf, and then with the love of a woman:

> Her soul is shut save to one thing – the love-quest consuming
> her.
> Fearless
> Crying, 'Ho, Servant, acquit me, the bound by Love's
> promises!
> Haste thou! He waits! I would go! Handle me lustily!'

Kipling is here finding a new image for the idea of the New Covenant of the New Testament: like Christ's love, the love of the woman in both poem and story, and the love of the cow for her calf in the poem, are both selfless, all-consuming and death-defying.

Throughout the story the man and the woman feel that their love calls into question conventional notions of reward and retri-bution. The story's title has several possible meanings: one is that illicit sexual love, when experienced in pain and anguish, can be part of a new Divine vision, something allowed as a mercy for those who suffer, because they 'suffer' love. At the beginning of the story the Archangels and Death debate 'the old Ruling': 'Who knoweth the spirit of man that goeth upward, and the spirit of the beast that goeth downward to the earth' (Ecclesiastes 3.21). Their conclusion – that only God knows what is 'spirit' and what is 'flesh', what is 'human' and what 'beast' – suggests that human codes of behaviour may well be more censorious than the Divine. It is as if the narrative is considering human ethics and morality *sub specie aeternitatis* and finding this inadequate. Indeed, in spite of the seemingly deterministic form of the narrative – the fixed 'Orders for Life': the punitive attitude of the angels, and the way human beings create their own Hells: 'Everything provided for according to their own imaginations' – here, as in 'On the Gate', Kipling seems to be trying to work out a new way of seeing the relationship between sin and suffering and Divine mercy. In 'Uncovenanted Mercies' Azrael says quite emphatically: 'My orders . . . are to dismiss to the Mercy.' Yet it is not Azrael who holds the key to the new vision. His attitude is at once too simple and too positive:

> My People [will have] . . . full advantages for self-expression and realisation. These will include impeccable surround-ings, wealth, culture, health, felicity, (unhappy people can't make other people happy, can they?) . . . That reminds me . . . My People's standards of comfort have risen, you know; and they're complaining of the – crudity of certain vital phenomena which lie within your provenance.

By contrast, the narrative suggests that those most worthy of Divine mercy, like the man and the woman whose 'state at the last shall be such as Evil itself shall pity', must demonstrate 'a high level of . . . passion and tenacity'. Significantly, it is the Guardian Angels, Ruya'il and Kalka'il, who understand love and suffering in human terms and perpetuate the new vision. Satan, Gabriel and Death still have a part to play here, but they are finally expelled: '[Ruya'il] looked as Kalka'il had done, straight into Satan's eyes, and: "Go!" she commanded . . . The three found themselves whirled into the Void.'

In 'A Madonna of the Trenches', as in 'The Wish House', we find 'Marvellous Mercy and infinite love' daringly associated with the vision of a mistress, but now also linked with the idea of the Resurrection. When Sergeant Godsoe hears from Bella Armine that she will shortly die of cancer, he times his suicide to correspond with the day of her death (the twenty-first of the month). He does this not only so that they can make love together in eternity, but so that they can make love together in death: 'an' he killin' 'imself so's to carry on with 'er for all Eternity – an' she 'oldin' out 'er arms for it! I want to know where I'm *at*!'

The tale is narrated by Godsoe's nephew, Clem, who witnesses the 'resurrection' of the lovers. Although he later discovers that Bella Armine died at home in London, he remains convinced that he did see her with Sergeant Godsoe in the trenches.

The most striking aspect of this story is its treatment of the physical body. There are repeated references to the frozen bodies of the dead soldiers used for making the trenches at 'French End an' Butcher's Row': 'There's nothing on earth creaks like they do! And – and when it thaws we – we've got to slap 'em back with a spa-ade!' But these are contrasted with the still-warm bodies of the dead woman and of Sergeant Godsoe, and with the hut warmed by the braziers. When Clem jokingly tells his uncle that he thinks he has seen Aunty Armine in the trenches, Godsoe is not surprised. Later he quotes to his nephew from the Church of England Service: 'If, after the manner of men I have fought with beasts at Ephesus, what advantageth it me, if the dead rise not?' The implication is that he and Aunty Armine will now be rewarded for their patient and unselfish love ('this must be only the second time we've been alone together in all these years'), and that they will consummate their love in death and throughout eternity: ' "Why, Bella!" 'e says. "Oh Bella!" 'e says. "Thank Gawd!" . . . Then he comes out an' says: "Come in, my dear"; an' she stoops an' goes into the dug-out with that look on her face – An' then 'e shuts the door from inside an' starts wedgin' it up.'

In this daring image Kipling brings together the two traditions of transcendental love, the 'sacred' and the 'profane' ('Mary' and 'Isolde'): a vision of perfect love, not in traditional terms as virgin love but as a love that is both spiritual and sexual: 'The reel thing's life an' death. It *begins* at death, d'ye see?' The persistent but puzzled allusions throughout the story to the resurrection of the body emphasize how incomprehensible these ideas are, particularly as they are expressed by the shocked and sceptical young narrator: 'What a bloody mix-up things are . . . if the dead *do* rise, why, what in 'ell becomes of me an' all I've believed in all me life?' Clem's apparent 'conversion' as a result of it all – ' 'Fore it ended, I knew what reel things reely mean!' – and at the same time his refusal to accept the full implications of what he has seen, is figured in the story's implicit equation of 'shell-shock' with 'belief', and shows the need for the intervention of the 'mercy and love' mentioned in the epigraph and in the story itself.

In 'A Madonna of the Trenches', as in 'The Wish House', the poem and the dramatic extract that preface and conclude the story also endorse the positive aspects of the uncovenanted and the illegal. Contempt for the conventional is expressed in the lightly mocking rhythms of 'Gipsy Vans':

> Unless you come of the gipsy stock
> That steals by night and day,
> Lock your heart with a double lock
> And throw the key away.

And in 'Gow's Watch' the princess who has seen perfect love is impatient with the demands of this world: 'God and my Misery! I have seen Love at last. What shall content me after?' Like the mysterious resurrection of the lovers in the story, these perspectives undermine what we would like to call 'reality': 'You see' – he half lifted himself off the sofa – 'there wasn't a single gor-dam thing left abidin' for me to take hold of, here or hereafter. If the dead *do* rise – and I saw 'em – why – why *anything* can 'appen. Don't you understand?'

In 'The Gardener' the emphasis is once again on the uncovenanted and the unconventional. Helen Turrell brings Michael, her illegitimate son, back to the village where she has always lived, and is obliged to pretend that he is her nephew. At the beginning of the story Kipling shows how the internalizing of love and the struggle to contain and measure it against conventional standards fracture the relationship between mother and son. They both suffer; they inflict pain on each other, and Helen feels a terrible sense of isolation because of her need to sustain the pretence outwardly, while strengthening their relationship in private. When Michael is six years old he is allowed to call Helen 'Mummy' at home. She perpetuates the lie by explaining to her friends and neighbours that Michael does this because she feels he must miss having a real mother. When Michael discovers this he feels angry and betrayed: 'You've hurted me in my insides and I'll hurt you back. I'll hurt you as long as I live.' Twelve years later Michael's sudden death in the war drives Helen even further into herself. Her particular circumstances prevent her from expressing her sorrow or from finding relief in the public rituals devised to meet it. Like the speaker in the poem that follows the story, she finds the intense inwardness of grief becomes an obsession, a secret 'burden':

> One grief on me is laid
>   Each day of every year,
> Wherein no soul can aid
>   Whereof no soul can hear:
> Whereto no end is seen
>   Except to grieve again –
> Ah, Mary Magdalene,
>   Where is there greater pain?

In the story itself Helen's inner distress is mirrored in the surreal quality of her perceptions, which are at once disturbed and psychologically acute: the village of Hagenzeele becomes 'a razed city full of whirling lime-dust and blown papers'; the Military Cemetery a 'waist-high wilderness as of weeds stricken dead, rushing at her'. Like a shell in a munitions factory – 'the wretched thing was never left alone for a single second' – she feels as if she is being 'manufactured' by the processes of grief. However, as in the stories of breakdown and neurosis, and the shell-shock stories, this disorientation marks the beginning of the process of healing.

The degree of Helen's love and loss is measured at the end of the story against that of Mrs Scarsworth and is heightened by the comparison. The two women meet on a 'pilgrimage' to Hagenzeele Third War Cemetery in France. Mrs Scarsworth's case is remarkably similar to Helen's. She too has been isolated by her own illicit love and oppressive lying: 'When I don't tell lies I've got to act 'em and I've got to think 'em always.' But there is something distasteful in her 'commissions' to take photos for other bereaved relatives, and in her attitude to the dead. Despite Mrs Scarsworth's later confession – 'there's *one*, d'you see, and –

he was more to me than anything else in the world' – it seems that
her love and grief are self-centred, even superficial, and cannot be
shared or alleviated by Helen's instinctive sympathy. By contrast,
complete acknowledgement of Helen's love and grief is registered
at the end of the story. Unable to find Michael's grave among the
twenty-one thousand of Hagenzeele Third, she seeks help from
the only other person present, 'evidently a gardener':

> She went towards him, her paper in her hand. He rose at her
> approach and without prelude or salutation asked: 'Who are
> you looking for?'
>
> 'Lieutenant Michael Turrell – my nephew,' said Helen
> slowly and word for word, as she had many thousands of
> times in her life.
>
> The man lifted his eyes and looked at her with infinite
> compassion before he turned from the fresh-sown grass
> toward the naked black crosses.
>
> 'Come with me,' he said, 'and I will show you where your
> son lies.'
>
> When Helen left the Cemetery she turned for a last look. In
> the distance she saw the man bending over his young plants;
> and she went away, supposing him to be the gardener.

Here both context and wording recall John 20.15: 'Jesus saith
unto her Woman, why weepest thou? whom seekest thou? She,
supposing him to be the gardener, saith unto him, Sir, if you have
borne him hence, tell me where thou has laid him, and I will take
him away.' Christ is seen here helping without being known, and
the substitution of the word 'son' for 'nephew' suggest that the
lifting of the burden depends upon an imaginative understanding
of the inner person not possible in conventional human terms,
and requires Divine love and understanding. At the same time,
however, such is the distortion of narrative created by the
language of the lie that the reader remains uncertain of Michael's
relation to Helen, and of the exact importance of the gardener's
words at the end of the story. After the event, we realize how
often, like Shafiz Khan, the plausible villain of 'One View of the
Question', Kipling's narrators have 'ridden sideways . . . at the
wall of expression'.

Kipling's search for deeper understanding is a central concern of his fiction, but so too is his awareness of mysteries that cannot be explained, and experiences that cannot fully be understood. 'But the pain *do* count, don't ye think, Liz? The pain *do* count to keep 'Arry where I want 'im. Say it can't be wasted like', Grace Ashcroft begs Liz Fettley in 'The Wish House'. So strong in her love and devotion, she still fears betrayal by the very powers she has proven to be real. At the end of 'The Gardener', Helen Turrell's experience balances understanding and misunderstanding, gain and loss, for she leaves still 'supposing him to be the gardener'. The equivocation of tone here is reminiscent of 'They', the story of the loss of a daughter, echoed by this story of the death of a son. And how significant that in 'The Gardener', the accompanying poem ends on a note of certainty, while the story itself finishes on a note of poignant pathos. Together they reflect that fundamental ambivalence or 'two-sidedness' evident throughout Kipling's writings: for Mary Magdalene in the poem, who loves the lost and defeated Christ, there is the triumph of the Resurrection: but for Helen Turrell there is only the unknown lifting of the burden of grief in a world where the dead do not return.

Notes

1   It is possible that Kipling's ideas were influenced by the Catholic doctrine of the 'Way of Exchange'. See Griffiths (1966, pp. 156–7): 'Of all the doctrines related to suffering which were preached at the time, that of vicarious suffering or mystical substition was the one which held the attention of Catholic writers . . . In taking on these sufferings for the world, man is imitating and to a certain extent supplementing the sufferings of Christ on the Cross . . . People may take on suffering for the community in which they live, or for the salvation of those near and dear to them . . . In the cases of all these forms of expiation . . . an essential element is the free will of the sufferer.'

2   See Proverbs 13.12: 'Hope deferred maketh the heart sick.'

Select Bibliography

Apter, T. E. 1982: *Fantasy Literature: an approach to reality*. London: Macmillan.

Arnold, Edwin 1870, repr. 1978: *The Light of Asia*. London: Routledge and Kegan Paul.

—— 1891: *The Wonderful Adventures of Phra the Phoenician*. London: Chatto and Windus.

Auden, W. H. 1943: The poet of the encirclement. *New Republic*, 29, 579–581.

—— 1963: *The Dyer's Hand and Other Essays*. London: Faber and Faber.

Babbit, Irving 1931: Romanticism and the Orient. *Bookman*, 74, 349–57.

Baldwin, A. W. 1960: *The Macdonald Sisters*. London: Peter Davies.

Bayley, John 1976: *The Uses of Division: unity and disharmony in literature*. London: Chatto and Windus.

—— 1986: The false structure. *English Literature in Transition*, 29, 19–27.

—— 1987: The tall and the true. *Times Literary Supplement*, 317–18.

Bazely, Basil 1949: Freemasonry in Kipling's works. *Kipling Journal*, 92, 13–14.

Beerbohm, Max 1943: *Around Theatres*. London: Rupert Hart-Davis.

Bhabha, Homi 1984: Of mimicry and men: the ambivalence of colonial discourse. *October*, 28, 125–33.

—— 1985: Signs taken for wonders: questions of ambivalence and authority under a tree outside Delhi, May 1817. In F. Barker *et al* (eds), *Europe and its Others*, II, Colchester: University of Essex, 89–106.

—— 1986: The other question: difference, discrimination and the discourse of colonialism. In F. Barker *et al* (eds), *Literature, Politics and Theory: papers from the Essex Conference 1976–84*, London: Methuen, 148–72.

Birkenhead, Lord 1980: *Rudyard Kipling*. London: W. H. Allen.

Blavatsky, H. P. 1889: *The Key to Theosophy*. London: Theosophical Publishing Co.

Bodelsen, C. A. 1964: *Aspects of Kipling's Art*. Manchester: Manchester University Press.

Briggs, Julia 1977: *Night Visitors: the rise and fall of the English ghost story*. London: Faber and Faber.

Carr, Brother H. 1964: Kipling and the craft. *Transactions of the Quatuor Coronati Lodge*, LXXVII, 213–53.

Carrington, Charles 1955, repr. 1986: *Rudyard Kipling: his life and work*. London: Penguin.

Cohen, Morton (ed.) 1965: *Rudyard Kipling to Rider Haggard: the record of a friendship*. London: Hutchinson.

Collins, E. J. Mortimer 1874: *Transmigration* (3 vols). London: Hurst and Blackett.

Colvin, Ian D. 1938: This bore fruit afterwards. *National Review*, 120, 215–21.

Culler, Jonathan 1981: *The Pursuit of Signs*. Ithaca: Cornell University Press.

Dummelow, J. R. 1909: *A Commentary on the Holy Bible*. London: Macmillan.

Eliot, T. S. 1919: Kipling Redivivus. *Athenaeum*, no. 4645, 297.

—— 1941, repr. 1979: *A Choice of Kipling's Verse*. London: Faber and Faber.

Ellmann, Richard 1959: *James Joyce*. Oxford: Oxford University Press.

Ewing, Juliana Horatia 1886: *Mary's Meadow, and Letters from a Little Garden*. London: Christian Science Society.

Fanon, Frantz 1965: *The Wretched of the Earth* (transl. Constance Farrington). London: MacGibbon and Kee.

—— 1970: *Black Skin White Masks* (transl. Charles Lam Markmann). London: MacGibbon and Kee.

Fleming, Alice 1897: *A Pinchbeck Goddess*. London: Heinemann.

—— 1937: Some memories of my brother. *Kipling Journal*, 44, 116–21.

—— 1939: Some childhood memories of Rudyard Kipling by his sister. *Chambers Journal*, Series 8, 169.

Foucault, Michel 1967: *Madness and Civilisation*. London: Random House.

Freud, Sigmund 1919, repr. 1953: The uncanny. In James Strachey (ed.), *Standard Edition of the Complete Psychological Works of Sigmund Freud*, vol. 17. London: Hogarth Press.

Friedman, Susan Stanford, *Psyche Reborn: The emergence of H. D.* Bloomington: Indiana University Press.

Frost, Albert 1942: Rudyard Kipling's Masonic allusions. *Kipling Journal*, 63, 16–18.

George, Samuel (ed.) 1921: *The Origin and History of Reincarnation: a symposium.* London: Power Book Co.

Gibbs, Robert Mood 1925: Rudyard Kipling and the Bible. Unpublished M.A. thesis, Columbia University.

Gilbert, B. J. Moore 1986: *Kipling and 'Orientalism'.* London: Croom Helm.

Gilbert, Elliott L. 1972: *The Good Kipling: studies in the short story.* Ohio: University of Ohio Press.

—— (ed.) 1965: *Kipling and the Critics.* New York: New York University Press.

Gilbert, Sandra 1983a: Rider Haggard's heart of darkness. *Partisan Review*, 50, 444–53.

—— 1983b: Soldier's heart: literary men, literary women, and the Great War. *Signs*, 8, 422–50.

Green, Roger Lancelyn 1971: *Kipling: The Critical Heritage.* London: Routledge and Kegan Paul.

Gribbon, Robert B. 1954: The Bible, the Prayer Book and Rudyard Kipling. *Kipling Journal*, 109, 3–6.

Griffiths, Richard 1966: *The Reactionary Revolution: the Catholic revival in French literature, 1870–1914.* London: Constable.

Hanson, Clare 1985: *Short Stories and Short Fictions, 1880–1980.* London: Macmillan.

Harper's Bazaar 1901: Kipling's spiritual side. 34, 796–97.

Hastings, James 1908–26: *Encyclopaedia of Religion and Ethics*, vol. 10. Edinburgh: T. and T. Clark.

Hill, Edmonia 1888: The young Kipling. *Atlantic Monthly*, 157, 406–15.

Holmes, Richard (ed.) 1987: *Something of Myself.* London: Penguin.

Hopkins, R. Thurston 1915: *Rudyard Kipling: a character study. Life, writings and literary landmarks.* London: Simpkin, Marshall, Hamilton, Kent.

Howe, Irving 1982: The burden of civilisation. *New Republic*, 68, 27–34.

Humphreys, Christmas 1968: *Sixty Years of Buddhism in England.* London: Buddhist Society.

Husain, Syed Sajjad 1964: *Kipling and India: an enquiry into Kipling's knowledge of the Indian Sub-Continent.* Dacca: University of Dacca.

James, Henry 1900: Introduction. *Mine Own People.* New York: Hurst and Co.

JanMohamed, Abdul 1983: *Manichean Aesthetics: the politics of literature in colonial Africa.* Amherst: University of Massachussetts Press.

Jarrell, Randall 1980: *Kipling, Auden and Co. 1935–1964.* New York: Farrar, Strauss and Giroux.

Karlin, Daniel (ed.) 1987: *The Jungle Books.* London: Penguin.

Kipling, John Lockwood 1891: *Beast and Man in India. A popular sketch of Indian animals in their relations with the people.* London: Macmillan.

Kipling, Rudyard 1937: *Something of Myself. For my friends known and unknown.* London: Macmillan.

—— 1928: *A Book of Words.* London: Macmillan.

Leed, Eric J. 1979: *No Man's Land, Combat and Identity in World War 1.* London: Cambridge University Press.

Leonard, M. 1976: *Madame Blavatsky: medium, mystic and magician.* London: Regency Press.

Lewis, L. A. F. 1982: Some links between the stories in Kipling's 'Debits and Credits'. *English Literature in Transition*, 25, 74–85.

—— 1986: Delays and obscurities. *Kipling Journal*, 240, 53–5.

Macdonald, Frederika 1885: Buddhism and mock Buddhism. *Fortnightly Review*, 43, 703–16.

—— 1887: *Puck and Pearl: the wanderings and wonderings of two English children in India.* London: Chapman.

MacMunn, G. F. 1934: Kipling's use of the Old Testament. *Kipling Journal*, 32, 110–18.

Mallett, Phillip (ed.) 1987: *Limits and Renewals.* London: Penguin.

Melchiori, Georgio 1960: *The Whole Mystery of Art. Pattern into poetry in the work of W. B. Yeats.* London: Routledge and Kegan Paul.

Messenger, N. P. and Watson, J. R. (eds) 1974: *Victorian Poetry.* London: Dent.

O'Connor, Frank 1965: *The Lonely Voice: A study of the short story.* London: Macmillan.

Olcott, H. S. 1932: *Old Diary Leaves: the true story of the Theosophical Society.* Madras: Putnam's Sons.

Parker, W. B. 1898: The religion of Mr Kipling. *New World*, 65, 662–70.

Parry, Ann 1985: Reading formations in the Victorian press: the reception of Kipling 1888–1891. *Literature and History*, 2, 254–63.

Regardie, F. Israel 1932: *The Tree of Life: A study in magic.* London: Rider.

Rhys Davids, T. W. (transl. 1880): *Buddhist Birth Stories; or, Jataka Tales. The oldest collection of folk-lore extant. Being the Jatakatthavannana.* London: Trübner.

Rilke, R. M. (transl. J. B. Leishman and S. Spender) 1948: *Duino Elegies.* London: Hogarth Press.

Robson, W. W. 1964: Kipling's later stories. In Andrew Rutherford (ed.), *Kipling's Mind and Art*. London: Oliver and Boyd.

Roskies, D. M. E. 1982: Telling the truth in Kipling and Freud. *English*, 31, no. 31, 1–17.

Ross, Angus 1987: *Kipling 86*. Brighton: University of Sussex Library.

Rouse, W. J. 1964: The literary reputation of Rudyard Kipling. Unpublished PhD thesis, University of New York.

Rutherford, Andrew (ed.) 1964: *Kipling's Mind and Art*. London: Oliver and Boyd.

Said, Edward 1978, repr. 1985: *Orientalism*. London: Penguin.

Sandison, Alan 1964: Kipling: the artist and the Empire. In Andrew Rutherford (ed.), *Kipling's Mind and Art*. London: Oliver and Boyd.

Sangharakshita, B. 1956: Buddhism in the modern world. In P V. Bapat (ed.), *Two Thousand Five Hundred Years of Buddhism*. Delhi: Publications Division, Ministry of Information and Broadcasting.

Sewell, Winifred 1935: Kipling's psychic phenomena. *Kipling Journal*, 35, 87–96.

Shepherd, Michael 1985: *Sherlock Holmes and the Case of Dr Freud*. London: Tavistock.

Sinnett, A. P. 1881: *The Occult World*. London: Trübner.

—— 1883: *Esoteric Buddhism*. London: Trübner.

Smith, B. A. 1926: Some Masonic references in Rudyard Kipling's works. *Transactions of the Somerset Master's Lodge*, 1–43.

Sullivan, Zohreh T. 1984: Kipling the nightwalker. *Modern Fiction Studies*, 30, 217–35.

Sunderland, Jabez T. 1899: The religion of Mr Kipling. *New England Magazine*, 20, 604–12.

Tompkins, J. M. S. 1959: *The Art of Rudyard Kipling*. London: Macmillan.

Trotter, David 1984: Review of Brian Clark, *Kipling*. *Times Literary Supplement*, 667.

Ward, Harry 1900: The religion of Mr Kipling. *Methodist Review*, 82, 262–9.

Weygandt, Ann 1939: *Kipling's Reading and its Influence on his Poetry*. Philadelphia: University of Pennsylvania Press.

White, Allon 1976: *The Uses of Obscurity: the fiction of early Modernism*. London: Routledge and Kegan Paul.

Wilde, Oscar 1890 repr. 1971: The true function and nature of criticism. In Roger Lancelyn Green (ed.), *Kipling: The Critical Heritage*. London: Routledge and Kegan Paul.

Wilson, Edmund 1923, repr. 1942: *The Wound and the Bow*. London: Secker and Warburg.

—— 1926: Kipling's 'Debits and Credits'. *New Republic*, 12, 194–5.

Index